Protecting Your Child
In an X-Rated World

FOCUS ON THE FAMILY®

Protecting
Your Child
In an X-Rated World

*What you need to know
to make a difference*

Frank York & Jan LaRue

TYNDALE

Tyndale House Publishers, Inc.
Wheaton, Illinois

PROTECTING YOUR CHILD IN AN X-RATED WORLD
Copyright © 2002 by Frank York and Jan LaRue. All rights reserved.
International copyright secured.

Library of Congress Cataloging-in-Publication Data

York, Frank.
    Protecting your child in an X-rated world / by Frank York and
Jan LaRue.
        p. cm.
Includes bibliographical references.
    ISBN 1-56179-907-6
    1. Children and sex. 2. Mass media and children. 3. Pornography.
4. Internet and children. I. LaRue, Jan. II. Title.
    HQ784.S45 Y67 2002
    363.4'7—dc21

                                                        20001007364

A Focus on the Family book published by Tyndale House Publishers,
Wheaton, Illinois.

Contents

꒤꒦

INTRODUCTION

The Death of Innocence

The two of us feel urgently the desire to help parents protect their children from pornography, because *both of us have personally suffered from its effects.* We know what pornography does to people, and that's why we're convinced that parents need to do everything they can to guard their children from it. This is increasingly difficult in our sex-saturated (or "X-rated") culture, but a concerned and informed parent *can* take positive steps that *will* make a difference.

When we first discussed the idea of coauthoring this book, we had no idea we had undergone similar exposures to pornography during our preteen and teen years. Our initial experiences came shortly after *Playboy* hit the newsstands in 1955. Both of us became victims

1

of pornography but in different ways. Let us relate our stories briefly so you will understand why we feel so strongly that parents must save their children from the scourge of porn.

JAN'S STORY

Having studied the spread of pornography in our culture for more than 10 years, I know that most child molesters use porn to fuel their desires before acting out their fantasies on children.

One day when I was only four or five years old, I went to a movie with my parents. My mother sat in the middle, between my dad and me. Then a man wearing a three-piece suit, carrying his hat in his hand, came into the theater. The auditorium was nearly empty, yet he sat down right next to me. My parents didn't even notice, but as young as I was, I thought, *Something is wrong here.*

With my mother and father sitting right next to me in the darkened room, this man kept putting his hand up my legs. I would knock his hand away and move closer to my mother until I was practically in her lap. She kept whispering to me, "Sit back, sit back."

After we left the theater, I told my mom and dad what this man had done, and they understandably got very upset that such a thing could and did happen. Yet that is the brazenness of a pedophile.

At the age of five, I was molested by the father of my baby-sitter.

Then, not long after my parents divorced, my mother remarried and we moved to a place in the country. My stepfather's brother lived with his wife and three sons not far from our home. My stepuncle molested me repeatedly and violently for two years when I was seven and eight, using his three sons to hold me down. He actually threatened to kill me if I told anybody about it. I kept silent, because I believed his threat was serious. (Since I lived on a farm, he could have killed me any number of ways and made it look like an accident.)

During that same period, my elementary school principal tried to molest me one day while driving me home when I'd missed the bus after school.

By the time I was eight years old, I had been molested by four men.

In high school I got involved with a bad crowd, and by age 15 I had a serious drinking problem. I also dated older boys and became sexually promiscuous. I didn't realize that I was displaying the classic symptoms of a sexually abused child.

In 1956, in my senior year of high school, I quit school and started working for a lawyer, a stockbroker, and a CPA who shared office space. Part of my job each month was to go out and purchase the latest copy of *Playboy* magazine. When I'd bring it back to the office, the men would invite some of their business associates over. We'd lock the office doors, I'd make them drinks, and we'd look through *Playboy* together. This went on month after month, and I was unwittingly being desensitized to what we were viewing.

One afternoon, after I'd had too many drinks, these men started telling me that I was far more beautiful than the women in the magazine and should be photographed. "Coincidentally," one of them had a camera with him. They convinced me to disrobe and pose for them. All those men are probably dead today, but I still wonder if someone doesn't yet have those pictures. To this day, it's painful and embarrassing to think about what I allowed them to do to me.

Looking for the Wrong Things

I eventually married an older man. I aborted our first child but later gave birth to a beautiful girl. Within two years, we were separated and then divorced. I met my current husband shortly after my first marriage dissolved. We both found Christ together and have been together ever since.

The Practice of Law

I had wanted to become a lawyer since I was 10 years old, watching *Perry Mason* on TV. Through a miraculous series of divine interventions, I was able to attend law school, and I graduated from Simon Greenleaf School of Law in California's Orange County in 1985 and was admitted to the California Bar. In 1989, I went to work for the Western Center for Law and Religious Freedom, where we defended 500 pro-lifers who had been arrested during Operation Rescue's protests in Southern California.

In 1992, I accepted a position with the National

Law Center for Children and Families in their West Coast office. The center deals specifically with pornography issues. While there, I worked to tighten the laws against child pornography and obscenity and helped get a law passed in California banning sexually explicit news racks from children's access. I was with the law center until 1998, when I became the senior director of legal studies for the Family Research Council in Washington, D.C. My specialties at FRC are pornography, religious liberty, and judicial reform.

Fighting Pornography

I am fighting pornography not only because I was sexually exploited by men whose actions were fueled by it. More importantly, I'm fighting porn for the sake of our nation's children, who are becoming the primary consumers of pornography and will eventually suffer damaged relationships and other serious harm if they are not safeguarded by their parents or other caring adults.

Pornography is no longer confined to the sleazy combat zones of our major cities. *Porn is now invading your home.* If you have a computer and an Internet connection, your computer is a virtual pornography bookstore and peep show booth. Porn is also available on most cable TV systems. And it's probably accessible on the computers in your local library. Your child may also be exposed in your public schools. You cannot trust your cable TV provider, Internet service, school, or local librarian to protect your child from pornography. In many cases, these are your worst enemies. Some of these sources are actively *promoting* the distribution of porn.

FRANK'S STORY

My first exposure to pornography came in 1955, when I was 11. Our local Rexall drugstore, which was near my elementary school, began carrying *Playboy* and smaller "girlie" magazines. Starting to experience the stirrings of testosterone, I found the covers on these publications fascinating.

I was too frightened to peek inside the magazines in the store, but I wasn't too scared to begin stealing them. I'm ashamed to admit it, but I started to occasionally slip one of the smaller magazines inside a comic book I would buy and take it home to look at in my bedroom. Though too guilt-ridden to keep stealing for long and terrified at the thought of getting caught, I stashed my small supply of magazines under our house in a crawl space. Once in a while, I would slip out to look at them. In my preteen years, I wasn't exactly sure what I was looking at, but it was forbidden and stimulating, so I was enthralled by it.

Pornography was not widely accessible in those days or I might have become a seriously addicted child. I would struggle with the temptation to use pornography for decades as it was.

During my teen years, I was exposed to porn in a number of ways. One day, for example, while out jogging along a country road with several friends who were training for track and field, we came upon some tattered magazines that had been tossed from someone's car. These became treasured possessions until the guilt overwhelmed me and I threw them away. Another time, a friend and fellow football player found a stack of magazines in his older brother's room, and we fantasized about the women we viewed.

My first exposure to hard-core pornography occurred when I was in Vietnam. Two coworkers in my clerical unit operated a lucrative side business by buying porn films in Saigon and having us pay a fee to watch them in the barracks. I could endure only one film. It was a grossly degrading display involving multiple sex partners in unspeakable acts. Thirty years later, I can still recall those horrible images even though I wish I could erase them from my mind.

XPOSE

In 1980, I began working as a researcher/writer at the Christian Broadcasting Network on a documentary series on pornography called XPOSE. Our staff spent a year and a half working on five hour-long shows. XPOSE's team traveled all over the United States, interviewing prosecutors and pornography victims and filming inside porn bookstores and peep show booths. I did extensive research on pornography and its addictive effects. I spent most of my time working on a documentary dealing with child porn and sexually abused children. Efrem Zimbalist Jr. served as the host for my show, "They're Killing Our Children." We interviewed Sara O'Meara, head of ChildHelp, USA (then called Children's Village, USA), and Clifford Linedecker, author of *Children in Chains*, a sobering look at the world of pedophilia and child molestation.

Both from personal experience and from my work on XPOSE, I know how dangerous pornography is. *But what Jan and I experienced during the mid-1950s is nothing compared to the availability of porn to children today.*

THE PORN THREAT TO YOUR CHILD

The two of us attended an antipornography conference in Cincinnati in April 2000. We both came away from it wondering if any parents could truly protect their children. Smut has so permeated our culture that it is available everywhere.

As a parent, can you safeguard your child in the sense of keeping him from *ever* seeing porn? Probably not. *But there is hope for you.* We believe you *can* protect your child in the sense of teaching him what God's Word says about wholesome and pure sexuality. You *can* build in him an understanding of and aversion to pornographic images and temptations. You *can* make it as difficult as possible for him to have access to porn in your home or neighborhood. And you *can* help protect your community by working to eliminate pornographic materials from your mini-marts, libraries, bookstores, and airwaves.

On the other hand, if you do nothing, your child is almost guaranteed to be exposed to pornography and morally tainted by it.

By reading this book, however, you've obviously decided to take action to protect your child. Good for you. Be forewarned, though: We're going to discuss unsettling and sometimes graphic materials in this book. You may be offended at some of what we say. But you must understand what your child is being exposed to—by friends, your local library computers, or your public schools. If we can alarm and energize you to do something about this moral scourge, we will have done our job.

Frank York and Jan LaRue, August 2001

CHAPTER ONE

The Danger in Pornography

Even in our Western culture that is increasingly tolerant of all things sexual, there's still a recognition among most people—whether Christian or not—that pornography is inherently bad or improper. But is it really harmful to individuals or society? After all, many men have seen a racy magazine or movie at some time and are hardly sex addicts by most definitions, let alone sexual criminals. Isn't it just a part of "Boys will be boys"? Groups like the American Civil Liberties Union and the American Library Association even defend porn vigorously as constitutionally protected free speech.

So, is pornography truly something that should have parents concerned? In a word, *yes*.

As you will soon see, children are being exposed to porn earlier than ever. And when they're exposed at whatever age, their thinking can be terribly distorted and their emotions damaged. They can become addicted and, in extreme cases, start acting out what they've seen. There's also the growing danger that they will be harmed by someone else whose own thoughts and actions have been corrupted by pornography.

If you're tempted to think that we might be exaggerating the scope of the problem, please read through the rest of this chapter, where we discuss each of the dangers mentioned in the preceding paragraph. But just for starters, consider the following:

◆ Dr. Mark Laaser, executive director and cofounder of the Christian Alliance for Sexual Recovery (and himself a former porn addict), reported to a committee of the U.S. Congress, "Pornography has the ability, according to all psychological theory, to program children early. We are now seeing research that is telling us that, whereas in my generation of men, the average age a person first saw pornography was age 11, now it's age five. A child who has the ability, and we're teaching them in school to do this, can get into these [Internet porn] sites very easily—four, five, six, seven year olds now are seeing things that in my extensive history with pornography I never saw. Pornography that is being seen is violent. It is degrading. It humiliates people, and it's teaching our children very immature, immoral, and damaging roles about themselves.

"All psychological theory would certainly confirm

that this kind of material, even if it's in its softest form, has the ability to affect a child's attitude, sexual orientation, and sexual preferences for the rest of their life. Internet pornography also can become very addictive. Addiction is progressive, and leads to more destructive forms of sexual acting out later in life."[1]

♦ A 1999 survey conducted by the Yankelovich polling firm discovered that more than 50 percent of teens admit to visiting pornography Web sites. Of the teens surveyed, a staggering 79 percent said they had found porn on their school or library computer. This figure is up 70 percent from 1997—just two years earlier. In addition, 67 percent said they access porn at home, and 64 percent said they also used a computer at a friend's house to access porn sites.

One of the most serious statistics from this study is that 75 percent of *parents* who were surveyed claimed that they knew "everything" or a "fair amount" about what their kids were looking at on the Internet. *That reveals a glaring ignorance on the part of parents about what their children are actually seeing on the Web.*[2]

♦ Children are also being hustled for sex by predators who stalk the Net. In June 2000, the National Center for Missing and Exploited Children released "Online Victimization: A Report on the Nation's Youth." The survey of 5,001 youth found that 19 percent of 10- to 17-year-olds reported getting unwanted sexual advances on the Net in the year preceding. It is believed that 48 percent of these cybersex advances were made by persons *younger* than 18. Sixty-six percent of those reporting a sexual advance were female. Seventy percent of the incidents occurred when the child was at home on his computer; 65 percent occurred while the youth was in a chat room; 24 percent came from an instant message.

♦ In addition, 25 percent of those in the "Online Victimization" survey said they had received "unwanted exposure to pictorial images of naked people or people having sex." The study says this represents an estimated 5.4 to 6.4 million children. Of the unwanted exposures, 71 percent occurred while the child was searching or surfing the Net, and 28 percent happened when opening an E-mail or clicking on links in an E-mail. Sixty-five percent of these incidents occurred at home, 15 percent in schools, and 3 percent in libraries.[3]

WARPED PERCEPTION: THE CENTERFOLD SYNDROME

Just how does pornography harm those who are exposed to it? The most common damage, the one that affects everyone who views porn, is that it warps the person's perception of people, relationships, and sex. It creates desires and expectations that make healthy intimacy nearly impossible.

Psychologist Gary R. Brooks gave this problem a name: the Centerfold Syndrome. Brooks, assistant chief of psychology service at the Department of Veteran

Affairs in Temple, Texas, said this syndrome makes men (and now boys) who view pornography incapable of entering into a healthy, long-term relationship with a woman.

In his 1996 book *The Centerfold Syndrome*, Brooks listed five characteristics of this emotional disorder:

♦ **Voyeurism**. The person prefers to look at women rather than interact with them. Our culture's promotion of sexualized images of women creates an obsession with visual stimuli—to the exclusion of real relationships.

♦ **Objectification**. Women become objects to be rated by size, shape, and harmony of body parts. Only those parts that give a man sexual satisfaction matter.

♦ **Validation**. Men (or boys) who become obsessed with the perfect women shown in pornography only feel masculine when they are with beautiful women. And the desirable companion maintains this man's interest only until she becomes less than perfect— through aging, childbirth, or other changes. A woman's value is judged solely by her attractiveness, not by her character.

♦ **Trophyism**. Males who are obsessed with pornography view beautiful women as trophies to be displayed, as property and conquests.

♦ **Fear of true intimacy**. Pornography's false images of women create a loneliness and a fear of real intimacy. The nude image on the paper or in the video has no expectations and no personality and can give nothing but sexual stimulation. The male ends up being robbed of his ability to relate emotionally or spiritually to a woman.

According to Dr. Brooks, "We have to challenge the idea that [pornography] is harmless." The Centerfold Syndrome can have devastating effects on impressionable boys and men who consume pornography.[4] In a speech before the American Psychological Association in August 1996, Brooks said that the Centerfold Syndrome is contributing to rising divorce rates, spousal abuse, and boredom and dissatisfaction in marriage.

Dr. Brooks began studying the impact of soft-core pornographic images in magazines like *Playboy* when he noticed his own attitudes changing toward his wife. Growing up, he had learned many of his ideas about women by gazing at pornographic magazines. His earliest relationships with women frequently failed because he was always looking for the "perfect" woman—the fantasy woman displayed in those magazines. He would break off relationships because of his girlfriends' flaws.

After 15 years of marriage, he began noticing himself losing interest in his wife because she was "getting old." At that point he realized he had to let go of his porn-induced fantasy image of the perfect woman.

Because of that experience and the professional research he has done, Dr. Brooks is deeply concerned about the impact pornography is having on preteen and teenage boys today. In an interview with a reporter from the *Chicago Tribune* in 1997, Brooks observed, "Boys learn that they become men by desiring strangers, women they don't even know. They don't learn to feel comfortable in relationships with real girls." He noted that pornography teaches boys that sex is only for recreation instead of a way for two people to express love for each other. Pornography "is not harmless. Once boys become sexual, they learn to see their bodies as sex machines."[5]

Dr. Brooks's analysis of the harm done by the Centerfold Syndrome is supported by the work of researcher Debbie Then. A survey of young men in the Stanford University School of Business Administration showed that their favorite magazines were *Playboy* and *GQ* (*Gentlemen's Quarterly*). According to Then, these consumers of pornography were critical of women who were overweight, and they wanted their sexual companions to look like the *Playboy* centerfolds. Her findings, said Then, "confirm women's worst fears that first and foremost they are judged by appearance and that their intelligence is secondary in importance. The men who view these magazines say they are more critical of real-life women—and that's even when they are aware that the pictures they're looking at are airbrushed and altered."[6]

In another study, Dr. Reo Christensen of Miami University in Ohio found that pornography leaves the impression with its viewers that sex has no relationship to privacy; that sex is unrelated to love, commitment, or marriage; that bizarre forms of sex are the most gratifying; that sex with animals is especially desirable; and that irresponsible sex has no adverse consequences.

In yet another study, Professors Dolf Zillman of Indiana University and Jennings Bryant at the University of Houston found that repeated exposure to porn results in a decreased satisfaction with one's sexual partner, the partner's sexuality, and the partner's sexual curiosity; a decrease in the value placed on faithfulness; and a significant increase in the perceived importance of sex without attachment.[7]

One person who learned firsthand the danger of the Centerfold Syndrome was a 34-year-old woman, married 14 years to a minister. She discovered he was seeking sexual satisfaction from pornographic Web sites. "How can I compete with hundreds of anonymous others who are now in our bed, in his head?" she asked in despair. "Our bed is crowded with countless faceless strangers, where once we were intimate."[8]

The bottom line is that boys and men who are exposed to pornography are socialized to view women as sex toys and body parts, not as human beings made in the image of God. These males then find it difficult to form lasting, healthy relationships with real girls. If these males marry, they will frequently be dissatisfied with their wives because they can never compare with the fraudulent images and behaviors of women who appear in pornographic magazines, videos, and Internet sites. Thus, by turning women into sex objects and creating unrealistic expectations in men, pornography destroys marriages and normal relationships between men and women.

AN EASY ADDICTION

A second serious danger posed by pornography is that the person using it will become addicted, with all the attendant problems associated with other kinds of addiction.

Sex addiction is a relatively new category of addiction, though the problem certainly isn't new. It is, however, growing at an alarming rate. For example, a Christian counselor in Dallas reported that the number of clients he sees who are addicted to pornography has risen significantly during the last 10 years.[9] Christian counselor Rob Jackson is seeing an increasing number of pastors who are secretly involved in pornography.

The Internet is compounding the problem and creating a whole new generation of sex addicts. Charles Colson has called Internet pornography "spiritual crack cocaine," and indeed it is. In 2000, Focus on the Family conducted a survey with the respected Zogby International polling firm on the Internet surfing habits of Americans. The results indicate that 1 out of 5 American adults may have looked for sex sites on the Internet. Of those surveyed, 31 percent of the men said they had visited sex sites. Focus also found that 17.8 percent of those who claim to be "born again" Christians and 18 percent of those who are married have visited sex sites.[10]

In March 2000, researchers from Stanford and Duquesne Universities released the results of a study of people (ranging in age from 18 to 90) who filled out an

MSNBC Web site survey. The questionnaire had asked them how much time they spend each week in the pursuit of sexually oriented Internet sites and the effect it had on their conduct. Of the 9,265 completed responses, 96—about 1 percent—fit the researchers' definition of a "cybersex compulsive," a person driven to find sexual materials on the Internet. To be so categorized, the person had to spend at least 11 hours a week visiting sexually oriented sites. We think that many hours is way too high in defining someone as a cybersex compulsive, but it certainly indicates the depth and seriousness of the problem.

Based on the survey results, it is estimated that 20 million people visit sex sites each month. If the questionnaire results are accurate, at least 200,000 of those visitors would be considered Internet sex addicts. *And this figure doesn't include the numbers of children who are becoming addicted because of the Internet.*[11]

The seriousness of cybersex addiction was highlighted in an article published in the *New York Times* in May 2000. According to Dr. Mark Schwartz with the Masters and Johnson clinic, "Sex on the Net is like heroin. It grabs them and takes over their lives. And it's very difficult to treat because the people affected don't want to give it up."

Dr. Al Cooper of Stanford noted that cybersex compulsives use the Internet as "an important way to their sexual acting out, much like a drug addict who has a 'drug of choice.'" Dr. Jennifer Schneider, associate editor of *Sexual Addiction and Compulsivity,* is greatly concerned about the impact pornography is having on family life. In a survey she conducted, 91 women and three men in committed relationships said they had experienced serious adverse consequences, including broken relationships, because of cybersex addiction.

Pornography and sexual addiction are commonly thought of as male issues. However, women are also succumbing to cybersex addictions. According to Dr. Cooper, most female cybersex addicts are single, but married women also get hooked. Women are less likely than men to visit pornographic Web sites, but they frequent sexually oriented chat rooms. Please don't misunderstand us. Not all chat rooms are pornographic, of course, but many women who get involved in romance-oriented chat rooms find themselves exposed to sexually explicit talk and potential seduction. Frank's two daughters, for example, logged on to a "Christian" dating chat forum one evening and were shocked at how many non-Christians had logged on to make obscene comments.

The Stages of Pornography Addiction

What stages does a pornography addict typically go through? Dr. Victor Cline is an expert on the subject by virtue of having treated hundreds of porn addicts, including children. Cline, a psychotherapist and specialist in family and marital counseling, says that a person usually progresses through four primary steps:

◆ **Addiction.** Repeated exposure to pornography gets the viewer hooked on it. The pleasurable experiences from it make him want to come back again and again. Males are especially vulnerable to porn addiction, perhaps because they have a greater capacity to fantasize.

◆ **Escalation.** The pornography addict eventually becomes bored with what he is viewing. He needs something more exciting to keep his interest. This frequently means more explicit, more sexually deviant, and even violent pornographic images, some involving the torture and mutilation of women. Dr. Cline has counseled many couples where the husband became so addicted to porn that he preferred it to making love with his wife.

◆ **Desensitization.** As the person continues to view pornography, what he once viewed as shocking or repulsive eventually seems normal and commonplace. The sexual activity depicted in the porn becomes legitimized in the person's mind. He develops the idea that everyone is doing this, so it must be okay.

◆ **Acting Out Sexually.** The final stage is not one that every addict goes through, but it is frequently the end result of a full-blown sex addiction. At this stage, the person crosses the line from being simply a porn consumer to becoming an adulterer, a sex offender, a child molester, a rapist, or even a murderer. The addict wants to act out the behaviors seen in the pornography. These behaviors include: compulsive promiscuity, exhibitionism, group sex, voyeurism, frequenting massage parlors, having sex with minor children, rape, and inflicting pain on himself or a partner during sex.[12]

The steady downward process of becoming addicted used to take as long as five to 10 years, but the Internet has changed all that. The trip from curious user to full-blown porn addict has been shortened by years because of easy access to pornography through the Net. A child can become quickly—even instantly—obsessed with Internet porn and begin moving rapidly through the stages of addiction described by Dr. Cline. But even

The Eight-Year-Old Addict

Several years ago, a mother brought her eight-year-old son, Jason, to psychologist Rob Jackson for counseling. Jason had become obsessed with women's breasts, even his own mother's, and frequently whispered "breasts" under his breath. Whenever he was around women, he would try to look down their dresses.

Jason had been exposed to pornography by a group of boys at school who were buying and selling porn videos. One of the boys had two working parents, so these kids routinely went to his house to watch movies unsupervised. Jason was gradually becoming addicted to pornography.

As Jackson worked with Jason, he tried to rule out every other possible emotional problem, including an obsessive-compulsive disorder, before giving a diagnosis of sex addiction. Yet the more Jackson probed into the boy's behavior, the more obvious it became that this child was a classic sex addict. During the diagnostic period, Jason's mother brought her husband to a meeting in an attempt to get him emotionally involved in the healing process. The husband, however, didn't think his son had a problem and refused to allow any further therapy. As far as Jackson knows, this boy has never been helped to overcome what could become a lifelong sexual addiction.

when the process is slower, the downward progression is inevitable if the child continues to expose himself to pornographic images.

How long does each stage last? It depends on the child and his particular vulnerability. If a child "acts out," however, a parent can be reasonably sure that he has gone through the previous stages that lead to a serious addiction.

Why and How Pornography Is Addicting

Pornography addiction is not just emotional or social. Like addictions to drugs or alcohol, there's also a physical component, as Dr. Cline explained in testimony before the Reagan Administration's Attorney General's Commission on Pornography. Porn makes a permanent impact on the brain. According to Cline, "Research suggests that experiences at times of emotional (or sexual) arousal get locked in the brain by the chemical epinephrine and become virtually impossible to erase. These memories, very vivid and graphic in nature, keep intruding themselves back on the mind's memory screen, serving to stimulate and arouse the viewer."

Cline continued, "This may help explain pornography's addicting effect. These powerfully sexually arousing experiences become vivid memories which the mind 'replays,' stimulating the child again and again, suggesting the need for further stimulation.... Most evidence suggests that all sexual deviations and their variations are learned behavior.... Many sexual deviations occur (or are learned) through the process of masturbatory conditioning. Vivid sexual memories and fantasies are masturbated to, which at the moment of climax further reinforces their linkage in the brain and leads in time to the increased probability of their being acted out in real life behavior."[13]

Dr. Jeffrey Satinover is the author of *Homosexuality and the Politics of Truth*. In his discussion of sexual behaviors and the brain, he pointed out that "behaviors become increasingly strengthened through repetition. This strengthening physically alters the brain in a way that cannot be entirely undone, if at all; it is modified with great difficulty."

While Satinover was discussing the compulsive sexual behaviors of homosexuals, the principles apply to the use of pornography as well. Dr. Satinover noted that the pleasure areas of the brain are most intensely activated at the moment of sexual orgasm. The mechanism that produces this pleasure is a chemical called an "opioid," meaning opiumlike. Aside from the use of heroin, wrote Satinover, no other experience gives so much pleasure as sex. As a person repeatedly engages in a sexual behavior, whether homosexual sex or watching pornography, these opioids are released in his brain and reinforce the pleasurable behavior. As a person continues in a particular sexual practice, the desire to repeat it becomes deeply embedded. The repetitive behavior actually strengthens connections between nerve cells and increases the amount of tissue. In short, a sexual behavior can alter the brain chemistry and increase the brain tissue involved in providing a person with the pleasurable sensation.

Satinover concluded, "Once embedded, sexual fantasy life in particular *cannot* be erased." New fantasies may be learned on top of the old ones; and, on the other hand, a person may become motivated *not* to act on his sexual impulses. But the sexual images and memories will always be there in the brain.[14]

William Stanmeyer, author of *The Seduction of Society: Pornography and Its Impact on American Life,* discussed how a pornography addiction can affect a person's behavior and attitudes. According to Stanmeyer, "The user of pornography must divorce himself entirely from all inhibitions, sense of modesty, and feelings of shame about watching other people perform sexual acts. He must deny the cultural assumptions that condemn the voyeurism he indulges." And, said Stanmeyer, the person who engages in this behavior must eventually go from being a passive spectator to becoming a participant in pornographic acts. For example, while pornography does not "cause" crime, it changes a person's attitude toward sexuality and predisposes the person toward criminal acts. "Thus," wrote Stanmeyer, "the flow of causality is not that pornography *causes* anti-social or criminal conduct. Rather it is that pornography causes deviant *attitudes* which in turn cause or predispose to anti-social or criminal conduct. In other words, crimes happen more frequently because pornography predisposes criminals to tolerate and even enjoy such anti-social conduct."[15]

Research certainly bears this out. The antipornography group Enough Is Enough! recently published a special report that listed several studies on the negative effects of pornography on its consumers. In "Just Harmless Fun? Understanding the Harm of Pornography," they noted the following:

♦ A 1994 review of 81 separate studies on the effects of pornography concluded that "the empirical research on the effects of aggressive pornography shows, with fairly impressive consistency, that exposure to these materials has a negative effect on attitudes toward women and the perceived likelihood of rape."

♦ An analysis in 1995 of 24 different studies found that "violence within the pornography is not necessary to increase the acceptance of rape myths." The rape myth is a message that men get from repeatedly viewing pornography: Women secretly enjoy being raped by men.

♦ Another analysis in 1995 of 33 studies found that "violent content, although possibly magnifying the impact of pornography, is unnecessary to producing aggressive behavior."

♦ A 1989 review of a series of studies found that men who consumed pornographic materials had an insensitivity toward victims of sexual violence, trivialized rape as a criminal offense, trivialized child sexual abuse as a criminal offense, and had an increased acceptance of pre- and extramarital sexual activities. The report noted that men who consume pornography become "sexually callous" toward women.[16]

In short, porn addiction tends to make men believe the rape myth, become more sexually aggressive themselves, and grow insensitive to the suffering of the victims of sex crimes.

Pornography can even condition a person into learning deviant sexual behaviors. In a laboratory setting, for example, by showing his adult subjects erotic pictures, Dr. Stanley Rachman successfully conditioned 100 percent of them into developing a sexual fetish. The fetish (or sexual obsession) can be targeted at a particular body part or even inanimate objects. There are actually pornography magazines devoted to foot fetishes. (Yes, some individuals become sexually aroused by looking at another person's feet.) There are also far darker obsessions, including a fascination with the dead.[17]

I (Frank) recently conducted an experiment. Just to give you an idea of how perverted individuals can become, I did a search on the Internet for how many sites might be devoted to a discussion of necrophilia, the practice of having sex with dead people. I found at least 130 Web sites on *one search engine alone.* Although I didn't click on the link to any of the sites, the descriptions vividly portrayed the philosophy and practice of necrophilia. The link descriptions promised crime scene photos, morgue shots, and more. One described "cute necrobabes" as a featured attraction.

I also did a word search on *bestiality* and came up with hundreds of sites devoted to discussions of bestiality by self-named "zoophiles," including photo features on having sex with animals.

The most frightening thing about the Internet is

that addicted, mentally unstable individuals who are involved in sick sexual practices can now find one another and reinforce their deviant behaviors. They can also recruit others into their deviant lifestyles by setting up colorful Web sites.

How many children are accessing these sites? How many are becoming addicted to porn or even being conditioned into bizarre sexual deviancies by consuming these materials? With the worldwide reach of the Internet, millions of children may be drawn into these dark and perverted lifestyles.

A Former Porn Addict Tells His Story

In May 2000, the commerce committee of the U.S. House of Representatives heard testimony about the Justice Department's lax enforcement of federal obscenity laws under the Clinton Administration. Among others (including the author, Jan), the congressmen heard from Joseph Burgin, a former pornography addict.

Mr. Burgin explained how porn had destroyed his life and marriage. He noted, "I've lost everything that a man would hold onto to give himself meaning and perspective in life. Because of my involvement with pornography, I lost my marriage of 25 years. It also cost me the role of daddy, which I cherish, to my 9-year-old daughter. My involvement with pornography also cost me job opportunities in the career path of my calling and choice. In addition to those things, I've lost friends and trust and respect from many…. Because of my involvement in pornography, I feel I'm scarred. I'm handicapped. I'll move into my future with a limp. I'll always be affected because of years of involvement with it."

Burgin told the committee members that his own father had introduced him to pornography when he was a teenager, which began his struggles with it. His addiction accelerated when he discovered the Internet. "It [his addiction] took off and went to a completely different level, mainly because of its ease of access and it was so easy for me to hide, and to mask from my own family, from my wife, from my children."[18]

Clearly, pornography can be quickly, fiercely, and permanently addicting. And that addiction can ruin lives and families.

CREEPING CORRUPTION

Pornography distorts the perceptions and harms the relationships of even "normal" consumers. Even worse, it can grow into a debilitating, lifelong addiction. But worse still, when people descend to the final, "acting out" stage of addiction, it can lead to the most vile of corrupt actions.

As just one example of what we mean, consider what happened to a 13-year-old girl. She told the following story at a press conference:

> You could say I'm a normal teenager, except for one fact. I'm a victim of pornography. When I was very

small, my real dad abused me while he was watching a pornographic video. I feel this in some way makes me different from other girls my age. I feel as if there is a place within me that is a dark place of unknown things. When I visit that place in my mind, I feel darkness, pain, fear, and confusion. This place makes me feel really sad. I cry sometimes. Other times, I just feel nothing. I feel as if something has been taken away from me and I will never get it back. Some days are all right; others are a struggle. On these days, I feel really sad, unloved and unwanted. I feel as if I'm not deserving of anything good. I feel lonely; I hurt on the inside. My mind spins in confusion. My heart feels as if it will break. One time I got so depressed I quit eating. I dehydrated and had to go to the hospital for IV fluids for five days. I was anorexic and had to start counseling. My counseling helped me to understand that I am angry, I am hurt and I'm sad and that's okay. I should be all of these things because I did lose a part of me. I lost my innocence of being a child. I lost my innocence to my real dad that chose to use me for his own self-fulfilling needs. The things he did to me happened while he watched pornography. What did I do to deserve this? I don't know. I don't understand. My mom says it's not my fault. I did nothing, but still I have to wonder. Wasn't I good enough or perfect enough? How could a daddy do this to his little girl? I don't know why. There are so many questions

I would like answered. I would like to know why
the courts didn't protect me and keep me safe. Why
is there such a thing as pornography? What good
does it do? It didn't do anything good for me. How
many other kids are hurting because of pornography? There have to be others like me.... [N]o one
can answer these questions for me. Some people
just wanted to ignore my questions, and me, and
my hurt.... But I can't help but wonder why was I
abused? How could adults sit quietly and let kids
like me be hurt?

Her mother then described how she had divorced
her porn-addicted husband, but a judge had forced her
to allow the girl to continue seeing her father on week-
ends. The abuse continued during these court-ordered
visits. Sadly, thousands of children could tell similarly
horrifying tales of losing their innocence to the impact
of pornography—and far more frequently these days as
a result of the spread of pornography on the Internet.

The Spread of Porn-related Child Molestation
Even the church is not immune to the effects of porn.
More and more Christians are developing secret
pornography addictions, which is leading to a growing
number of cases in which these men act out their sexual fantasies on children under their care. In mid-2000,
for example, parents in Middleton, Massachusetts,
learned that a church worker—a man they trusted—
had molested as many as 250 boys over a period of

years. The man had served as a youth worker, summer camp counselor, and Boy Scout volunteer.

Investigators found a list of the boys on the man's computer. These boys were between the ages of five and 14. The database contained graphic descriptions of each boy's body. Police also discovered dozens of pornographic magazines and videos, photos of naked boys, and inflatable plastic dolls he had used in seducing his victims. Investigators also found a hidden camera in the church where this man had served as a youth coordinator.[19]

In Pennsylvania, a preacher was arrested during the summer of 2000 after arranging a sexual encounter with a New Jersey teenager in an Internet chat room. The 14-year-old boy he thought he was going to exploit sexually was actually an FBI agent. At the same time, a New York priest was also arrested for trying to arrange a sexual encounter with a teenage boy.[20]

Not a day goes by without some newspaper account of a child being molested by an adult or a child molesting another child. What has happened in Arizona is becoming typical. Statistics issued in 1998 indicate that 70 percent of the sexual offenders in the state's prisons victimized children. Eighty percent of the physical exams done on sexual assault victims are on children. Of the 3,000 sex offenders in Arizona in 1998, 2,100 had targeted children. Of these, 30.8 percent attacked family members, 44.1 percent attacked a nonfamily acquaintance, and only 25.1 percent went after strangers.[21]

Statistics compiled by the antipornography group

Enough Is Enough! are also shocking. According to this group, approximately one in three girls and one in seven boys will be sexually molested before age 18. The typical molester will abuse more than 360 victims over his lifetime. In fact, according to Dr. Gene Abel at Emory University, the typical molester will successfully abuse from 30 to 60 children before he is caught the first time.

The Los Angeles Police Department's Sexually Exploited Child Unit studied child abuse cases between 1980 and 1989. They found that pornography was

---

Victims of the Internet

A missionary family returned from a developing nation not long ago. While overseas, this family subscribed to an unfiltered Internet service. Their 14-year-old son began surfing the Web for pornography sites, and he continued to access porn when the family returned on furlough. Two months after coming home, his mother walked into his room and found him molesting a six-year-old neighbor girl.

Horrified at what she'd seen, the mother immediately contacted the girl's family and apologized for what had happened. In addition, she contacted the authorities, and her son was required to go into a court-ordered sex addict treatment program. The mission board dismissed the couple as missionaries and removed them from missionary housing.

This tragedy might have been avoided if these parents had known the dangers of having unfiltered Internet service in their home. They are now working to rebuild their lives because of their son's obsession with pornography. In addition, a little girl was traumatized and could spend years in therapy to deal with her sexual abuse.

directly involved in 62 percent of the cases and actually found in the home of the molester in 55 percent of the cases. The report's author, Ralph W. Bennett, noted, "Clearly, pornography, whether it be adult or child pornography, is an insidious tool in the hands of the pedophilic population.... The study merely confirms what detectives have long known: that pornography is a strong factor in the sexual victimization of children."[22]

Rape Rates on Rise

Not only is pornography clearly an incitement to child molestation, but it also incites men to commit rape and other sexual violence against women. Rape has increased by 500 percent in the U.S. since 1960, a rise that parallels the growth of the pornography industry. Researcher Dr. W. Marshall published a report on the connection between pornography and rapists in the *Journal of Sex Research* in 1988. Marshall wrote that 86 percent of convicted rapists said they were regular users of pornography, and *57 percent admitted direct imitation of pornographic scenes when they committed rape.*[23]

In short, pornography is a teaching manual for rapists, providing visual models to use in committing their crimes. Not all rapists, of course, are porn addicts. Many are sociopaths who use violence to punish women, have power over them, or inflict pain upon them. Yet as we have seen, pornography use is closely related to the propensity of a man to act out his sexual fantasies by raping a woman.

The American Family Association's publication "A

Guide to What One Person Can Do About Pornography" contains additional alarming information about the relationship between pornography and sex crimes. For example:

◆ Detroit police Chief Herbert Case has observed, "There has not been a sex murder in the history of our department in which the killer was not an avid reader of lewd magazines."

◆ A study of "recreational killers" (individuals who kill for fun) by the National Institute of Mental Health reported that these killers are highly intelligent but are consumed with sadistic lust, and most "feed on pornography."

◆ Researchers Murray Straus and Larry Baron issued a report that found a high correlation between high rape rates and pornography use in both Alaska and Nevada. These researchers concluded, "The fact that sex magazine readership is strongly and consistently correlated with rape supports the theory that porn endorses attitudes that increase the likelihood of rape."[24]

WHERE PORNOGRAPHY IS TAKING MANY CHILDREN

With the easy access to pornography, children are becoming sexualized and addicted at earlier and earlier ages. As Dr. Laaser noted at the beginning of this chapter, not very many years ago, a child's first exposure to pornography was typically at age 11. Now it is down to five years of age. What does this mean to you as a parent? It means that your child is in danger of having his views of sexuality and relationships permanently warped, and of developing a sexual addiction before he even reaches his teen years—if he has access to pornographic materials. It also means that he may, like a growing number of kids, become a predator.

In the late 1980s and early 1990s, social workers, police, and juvenile court authorities began noticing a disturbing and growing trend among children and teenagers: the juvenile sex offender. The *Orange County (California) Register,* for example, reported in 1991 that the criminal justice system was seeing a growing number of young rapists. In California, the number of children ages 11-12 who were arrested for rape went from 17 in 1986 to 32 in 1990.[25] Nationally, 297 children were arrested for rape in 1986 and 346 in 1990. Many of these rapists began their criminal careers when they were eight or nine years old. A report in the *Philadelphia Inquirer* in 1993 noted that nearly half of the nation's child molesters were children. In addition, in 1983 there were only 22 juvenile sex offender programs nationwide; in 1993 that number had grown to 755. Today there are more than 1,200.[26]

More and more police departments are being overwhelmed by a growing number of child sexual abuse cases. The Akron, Ohio, police department, for example, has a seven-member juvenile division that is swamped by sex offense cases. In 1999, Akron police had to deal with 121 sex offenses involving child predators, including 65 cases of rape—double the number in 1997. During the second half of 1998, detectives faced an average of six new cases of juvenile sex abuse each day. It nearly overloaded the entire division.

One case involving a boy named Michael is typical. Michael's sexual urges began to be stirred on weekend visits to his grandparents' home in Cleveland. When he was sure they were asleep, he would stay up late at night, switching cable channels until he found adult movies. The images he saw fueled his sexual fantasies. He was also jolted to learn that his grandfather had molested his sister. "At first, I was mad," said Michael. "I was blaming it on my sister. That's when I committed my offense." He raped a four-year-old boy.

Judge Judith Hunter, a juvenile court judge in Summit County, Ohio, is deeply concerned about the trend she's seeing. According to Hunter, "We have .coming through juvenile court some of the most serious offenders I have ever seen." In an article in the *Akron Beacon Journal,* Hunter cited the case of a 17-year-old indicted on one count of rape and two counts of attempted rape. Hunter concluded that pornographic movies, TV shows laced with sexual innuendo, and music videos glorifying rape play a significant role in many of the cases she sees.[27]

A SERIOUS THREAT

Our goal in this chapter has not been to make you paranoid about pornography, but to help you become well-informed as you clearly confront this issue. Pornography is a serious threat to your child's spiritual and moral well-being. It's not something you can shrug off and pretend that it can have no impact on you or your family.

Prayer and vigilance are essential if you are to protect your child in this X-rated world. Don't expect a Christian school or your church to shield your child from exposure. Moreover, don't assume that allowing your child to associate only with other Christian children will keep him or her safe. Pornography can find its way into Christian homes, and if it's in the home, a child will find it.

In the next chapter, we'll show you just how widespread porn has become. Prepare to have your eyes opened wide.

CHAPTER TWO

The Pervasiveness of Pornography

༷

A mother in California recently discovered that her son had a briefcase full of pornography hidden under his bed. One of his neighbor friends had access to his father's supply of magazines and videos, and both boys were trading the material or selling it to buy videos or video games forbidden by their parents.

One night a few months ago, my wife, Barbara, and I (Frank) visited a Tower Bookstore in our hometown of Nashville, Tennessee. Shortly after Barbara began looking at some magazines, a 10- or 11-year-old boy walked up to her, opened a pornography magazine, and laughed as he said, "Look at these." He then threw the magazine onto a pile of books and kept laughing as he walked out of the store. When Barbara quickly closed the magazine, she was shocked to find that the back and front covers were just as explicit as what she'd seen inside.

Tennessee has a "harmful to minors" statute that requires sexually explicit magazines to have cardboard covers in front of them and to be kept out of the reach of children. Yet this boy had apparently had no trouble getting his hands on just such a publication there in a mainstream bookstore.

Children innocently surfing the Internet for harmless information can also find themselves exposed to pornography through a technological ploy called "mouse-trapping," akin to the hijacking of a car. Here's an illustration of how it works: The day after my wife's encounter with pornography in the bookstore, I logged on to the Internet to look for research papers on the effects of porn addiction. My search engine listed several dozen relevant sites, and I clicked on one that looked promising. It turned out, however, to be a porn site.

As the images loaded onto my browser, I clicked the *x* on the window to get out of it, but another window popped up with more pornography. As I tried to get out of this second site, a third appeared. Since it seemed this might go on indefinitely, I finally was forced to turn off the computer in order to break the connection.

With this technology, pornographers are frequently seizing control of children's browsers when they stumble upon porn sites. Each time the child attempts to get out, a new porn window appears. Page after page of sites appears. The more the child works to get out, the worse the situation becomes.

As these three incidents illustrate, pornography is readily available to children in many forms and many ways. Let's look at just how pervasive it has become.

WHERE KIDS CAN GET PORNOGRAPHY

Dial-a-Porn

Several years ago, before the Internet became the main source of pornography for children, dial-a-porn was one of the primary ways kids would be exposed to indecent materials. These sites are accessed through 900 numbers. Blocking devices have effectively removed this as a primary threat to children, but if your phone company doesn't have a blocking device available for your use, your kids can still hear sex talk over the phone. Most pornography magazines and hundreds of Internet sites offer dial-a-porn services.

Writing in *Pornography's Effects on Adults and Children,* Dr. Victor Cline, a therapist who treats pornography addicts, described interviewing a 12-year-old boy who once listened to a dial-a-porn service for nearly two hours from a pastor's church study on a Sunday afternoon. A few days later, he assaulted a four-year-old girl in his mother's day care center. According to Dr. Cline, this boy "had never been exposed to pornography before. He had never acted out sexually before and was not a behavior problem in the home. He had never heard of or knew of oral sex before listening to Dial-a-Porn. And this was how he assaulted the girl, forcing oral sex on her in direct imitation of what he had heard on the phone."

Cline said he later interviewed a number of children in Michigan where teenage boys had forced sex on younger females as a result of listening to phone sex messages.[1]

Pornographers also use 800 numbers to lure adults and children into accessing sexually provocative phone calls. These numbers are posted in Web sites, porn magazines, and porn newspapers available in street corner news racks (see section below).

Pornographic Baseball Cards and Comic Books

Yes, there are such things as pornographic baseball cards and comic books. And children don't have to go into adult bookstores to get them. If your community has a comic book store, your children might easily obtain sexually explicit comics and cards. The comics are often placed next to *Batman* or *Superman* comic books. The pornographic trading cards are next to baseball or football cards.

The most notorious porn comic book series is called the Cherry series. These are extremely hard-core materials. One of them is a spoof of *Back to the Future*. In this particular comic, the lead character, Cherry, goes back in time and has sexual relations with her mother. In addition, many of these comics contain depictions of bestiality, which is sex with animals. (In the world of pornography, any sexual activity is okay as long as it gives pleasure to the one engaging in it.)

Clerks in these stores don't usually monitor kids to control what they're looking at. Thus, if your kids frequent these stores, they may be exposed to hard-core pornographic materials teaching that perverted sexual activities are normal and acceptable. Your kids may be purchasing these materials and hiding them at home or trading them with their friends.

Pornographic Music/Lyrics

If your kids listen to today's popular music, they may be getting exposed to unhealthy messages through the lyrics. Rap groups are notorious for their pornographic descriptions of violent sex acts against women. In addition, groups like the Red Hot Chili Peppers are well known for their nudity on stage and for their indecent descriptions of sexual acts. White rapper Eminem sings about viciously killing his lover, telling her "Now bleed, b****, bleed."

Networks like MTV that air music videos are major marketers of sexually provocative and perverted sexual activities. Spend an hour or so watching MTV and you'll quickly discover the major themes: lust, Satanism, premarital sex, violence against women and authority figures, and anarchy.

Video Games

In May 2000, Simon & Schuster released a new video game called "Panty Raider," which requires young players to strip supermodels down to their underwear in order to save the world from an alien invasion. As long ago as 1993, video game companies were releasing "erotic video games" featuring sexually oriented situations, mixed with live performances. New Machine Publishing, for example, released "Dream Machine" in 1993. In this game, players are encouraged to go through different doors where they are exposed to various sexual fantasies.

E-mail Solicitations

If you're on the Internet often, you may have already received unwanted E-mails from pornographers. The free Microsoft service called Hotmail seems to have the greatest number of these unwanted come-ons. I (Frank) canceled my Hotmail account recently because I was receiving dozens of pornography-related messages a week. These E-mails usually have a clever heading on them to lure you into opening the message. Many contain links to porn sites. The pornographers, of course, don't care if children are exposed to these materials—in fact, they hope they will be.

Don't assume your child has been searching for porn sites simply because you receive a porn E-mail. The pornographers routinely scour the Internet for addresses and then conduct mass E-mailings to new names. If you have received these unwanted messages, you can block them and/or report them to the Internet service provider so they will be permanently blocked.

Public Libraries

Thanks largely to the efforts of the American Civil Liberties Union (ACLU) and the American Library Association (ALA), thousands of libraries across the U.S. have been turned into adult bookstores and peep show booths. Both organizations have vigorously opposed the use of Internet filtering systems on computers available for public use in libraries. They claim that filtering is a violation of "free speech," but what they're actually doing is allowing children to have access to the most dangerous forms of pornography imaginable.

The Family Research Council published a detailed report on how children are being molested and are becoming molesters as a result of pornography's being accessed on library computers. *Dangerous Access 2000 Edition: Uncovering Internet Pornography in America's Libraries,* written by former librarian David Burt, documents dozens of cases where children have been exposed to porn while at the library. In my foreword to this report, I (Jan) noted,

> While approximately 74% of public libraries
> provide some access to the Internet and related
> services through interactive computer services,
> only 15% of those libraries utilize some type of
> blocking technology on at least some of their
> public workstations.... *Dangerous Access 2000
> Edition* proves that library online services are
> being used by adults and children to access

illegal pornography, and that libraries are scenes
of public masturbation and other sex crimes,
often with full knowledge of library staff, some
of whom have refused to call the police.[2]

Here are just a few examples of how children are
being victimized by porn in libraries:

♦ In Grayville, Illinois, the director of the library
reported that "five teenagers/young men lost computer
privileges for accessing sexually explicit-pornographic
web sites.... Two of the young men actually entered the
library after hours to access these locations."

♦ In Broward County, Florida, a library staffer
reported that a "young man probably 13 or 14 years old
had accessed something having to do with sex with animals. He acted strangely, perhaps also masturbating."

♦ In Phoenix, a four-year-old boy was the victim of
an attempted molestation in a library restroom. A 13-
year-old who had been viewing pornography earlier
offered the boy 25 cents to engage in oral sex with him.

♦ In the Fort Vancouver, Washington, public library,
staffers were alarmed to discover that boys were masturbating in the restrooms after viewing pornography.

A former librarian in upscale Brentwood, Tennessee, said that her library is having problems with an
adult male who regularly views pornography on an
Internet-connected computer and doesn't seem concerned that young children can watch while he does so.
At the time of this writing, the library has unfiltered
computers. In an effort to decrease the accessing of porn

Winning the Fight for Filtering

As Focus on the Family's *Citizen* magazine reported in "Libraries Feel the Pressure," the local chapter of Citizens for Community Values (CCV) in Memphis, Tennessee, led a successful charge to filter library computers used by both children and adults. Here's the story:

"The battle began after a mother and her 15-year-old son happened upon a man masturbating as he viewed pornography in a suburban Memphis library. The mom reported the incident to the library and police. The offender's penalty? No access to the library for 60 days.

"Though local media didn't pick up the story, word did reach local county commissioners.

"'County government pays 25 percent of the funding for the library system,' said CCV Director George Kuykendall. 'When they held budget hearings for the public libraries, the county commissioners told them they would not give them any money till they came up with a plan for filtering the Internet.'

"Kuykendall and other CCV members continued to lobby the commissioners, presenting facts and figures supporting their position. They included the results of a CCV survey that showed three of four Memphis-area residents in favor of filtering.

"Come September 1999, Memphis and Shelby County Library Director Judith Drescher and the library board of trustees did a dramatic U-turn, electing to install filtering on each computer in the system's 23 branches. Essentially, the library decided to apply the same criteria to the Internet that it uses when adding books and videos to its collection, Kuykendall explained.

"'Libraries all across the country can use that same policy for the Internet,' Kuykendall said."

on these computers, the monitors were faced to the aisle on the assumption that porn users would be embarrassed to have other library patrons see what they were looking at.

The strategy hasn't worked, however, because porn users often don't care if others—even kids—see pornography. In fact, many of these sex addicts *want* children to view porn. In public libraries everywhere, pedophiles are now routinely accessing child porn sites.

Newspaper Racks

If your state does not have a law against the public display of pornographic newspapers in newspaper racks, your child can freely access these publications on street corners. Inside these newspapers are Internet porn sites, dial-a-porn numbers, and hard-core sexual content.

Cable and Satellite TV

Until recently, cable and satellite companies were required by law to block both the audio and video feeds of pornographic services like the Playboy Channel, Ecstasy, and The Hot Network or time-channel the programming from 10:00 P.M. to 6:00 A.M. Playboy, however, won a court decision in early 2000 that overturned the federal law requiring total blocking. The video of these channels is still scrambled (not totally blocked out), but the cable company is free to broadcast the audio. Children can see enough of the image to be sexually aroused, and the audio only adds to the seductiveness of the forbidden images.

One of the most serious threats to your child's sexual well-being is your local public access cable channel. Under current law, a person who wants to put a pornographic show on public access in prime time is free to do so—and it won't be scrambled.

Cable/satellite channels also frequently advertise sexually explicit videos with titles like *Wild Girls on Spring Break*. The ads show nearly everything but full frontal nudity. USA Network and E! run these often. One parent saw such ads running on a cable channel that was only one click away from Nickelodeon. We'll deal with these issues in more detail in a later chapter.

Network TV and Radio
Howard Stern, Jerry Springer, and Sally Jesse Raphael are only three of numerous TV and radio personalities who regularly feature pornographic or sexually provocative materials on their shows. Stern is a target of an American Family Association (AFA) effort to get sponsors to drop his programming. Stern's televised version of his CBS radio program on the E! network features vulgar sex talk and female guests who bare their bodies for Stern. (The AFA has described some of Stern's programming on its Web site.) While their private parts are blurred for the camera, these nearly-naked women engage in behaviors designed to arouse lust in the viewer. Stern is rabidly pro-abortion, anti-Christian, pro-homosexual, pro-pornography, and pro-pedophile. Springer and Raphael, for their part, regularly feature prostitutes, transvestites, and porno stars on their programs.

Jerry Springer was recently the host of an MTV special on the antics of college students on spring break in Florida. On this program, young women bared their breasts to a huge crowd. Young men removed their swimming trunks and ran naked across the stage. In another part of the program, young couples were squeezed into a telephone booth, where they raced to exchange swimming suits. A camera on top of the booth showed both males and females getting naked in the process.

Network television's sitcoms and dramas are also becoming more and more sexually explicit. Morality in Media (MIM), one of the oldest antipornography groups, published an in-depth study of network TV in 1998. In *TV: The World's Great Mind-Bender,* MIM noted, "Much of today's television is addicted to cheap sex the way a wino is addicted to cheap wine. And TV's casual sex is worse, because TV is omnipresent. You can avoid Skid Row in your travels, but TV's red-light district is camped out permanently in your living room."[3]

Shows like *Dawson's Creek, The Drew Carey Show, Friends, Spin City, Buffy the Vampire Slayer, NYPD Blue,* and *Will and Grace* all carry inappropriate sexual themes. (*Dawson's Creek* producer Kevin Williamson, for example, is a homosexual activist and the creator of the *Scream* film series. He has admitted that he puts pro-homosexual propaganda in his films and TV shows.) The plots of these programs regularly include the following: adultery, homosexual characters, sexual profanity, blasphemy, and, in the case of dramas, extreme violence. The producers and writers of these shows view themselves as "teachers" who are working to change our culture and our attitudes toward homosexuality, traditional sexual morality, and religion. Christianity is typically targeted for ridicule. Christian morality is, of course, a direct threat to those who wish to have total sexual "freedom" in our culture.

Films

Movies are awash in sexually inappropriate themes. For example, the PG-13 blockbuster *Titanic,* with teen heartthrob Leonardo DiCaprio and Kate Winslet, was seen by millions of teens and preteens. Yet how many parents knew beforehand that their children would be exposed to Winslet's bare breasts and implied sexual intercourse with DiCaprio in the back of a car in the ship's hold? What kind of moral message did *Titanic* send to our nation's children? *Premarital sex with someone you "love" is fine. If it makes you feel good, just do it and don't worry about the consequences.*

How many young men were sexually aroused to the point of acting out their fantasies on young women after viewing this film? How many girls lost their resolve and their virginity after watching this "romance"? We'll probably never know, and the film's producers certainly don't care.

If you've seen many recent movies, you've already learned that sexual content appears in the most unexpected places. There is no need for nudity in films, but producers and writers seem determined to drop in nude scenes whenever they can. Such a scene need not be related in any way to the plot of the movie, but it's there because a producer or writer *wants* it there.

Detailed Analysis

The respected public policy group Center for Media and Public Affairs (CMPA), based in Washington, D.C., issued a special report on sex in the media in March 2000. The report, "Sexual Imagery in Popular Entertainment," built upon research published previously by CMPA in late 1999. In this report, CMPA did a content analysis of 248 broadcast and cable TV programs, the 50 highest-rated made-for-TV movies during 1998-99, the 50 top-grossing movies released in 1998, and 495 airings of 189 different music videos that appeared on MTV during four randomly selected days of programming during 1998-99.

According to CMPA, "In all, the 843 pop culture products that we examined contained 5,152 separate scenes with sexual material. Nearly two-thirds of these (63%) consisted of visual images ranging from nudity to simulated intercourse; the remaining 37 percent appeared in spoken dialogue or song lyrics. Nearly three quarters of these scenes (72% or 3,732) consisted of 'soft-core' material, such as nudity, masturbation, sexual dysfunction, and exhibitionism; the remaining 28 percent (1,420 scenes), included 'hard-core' material involving sexual intercourse, oral sex, X-rated pornography, incest, etc."

The most sex-saturated network was NBC, with 22 sex scenes per hour. Basic cable averaged one sex scene every five minutes and one hard-core scene every 12 minutes. Lifetime had 13 hard-core scenes per hour, but Showtime is the king of sexual programming, with an astonishing 69 sex scenes per hour, including one hard-core scene every three minutes. In

The unspoken objective is to sexualize the audience. R-rated movies nearly always contain nude scenes. More and more PG-13-rated movies do also. No

❧ ───

addition, MTV took the prize for the most sexually explicit network with 93 sexual scenes per hour. One MTV video, "Anywhere," had 37 sexual scenes jammed into a three-minute segment.

With all the sexual activity being shown on TV and in movies, one would think the characters might experience some negative consequences—like sexually transmitted diseases and unwanted pregnancies. Not so, said CMPA. "One of the most striking things about the portrayal of sex in popular entertainment is how rarely it has any consequences for either the participants or any other characters. Out of 3,228 scenes showing sexual activity, including 135 scenes of simulated on-screen sexual intercourse, only eight pregnancies and not a single case of sexually transmitted disease resulted. Overall, 98 percent of these instances had no physical consequences of any sort."

Were there any emotional consequences of engaging in premarital sex? Not really. CMPA noted that "the absence of emotional and physical consequences was in keeping with the non-judgmental attitude toward sex that was usually exhibited by scripts and plotlines. Fully 95 percent of all instances of sexual activity elicited no clear moral or even prudential judgment. Two percent of all instances were specifically judged to be appropriate or acceptable behavior; another two percent were deemed unacceptable or inappropriate. But the overwhelming verdict of popular entertainment was that sex is neither right nor wrong; it just happens." You can download this report for more details at: www.cmpa.com.

matter how brief the scene, it leaves an impression and creates a lustful desire in the male viewer. In addition, sexualized violence in film is becoming a key influence in the rising tide of sex crimes committed by younger and younger children.

If you haven't already done so, you're going to have to become careful in monitoring what movies your children are allowed to see and what videos they're allowed to rent. Don't assume that a PG-13 or even PG rating means it's safe for your kids to view. Even a PG-rated film could contain nudity or sexually inappropriate themes.

Hotels and Motels

In most U.S. hotels and motels, pornographic channels are available on the in-room TV for a fee. Making matters worse, many of these movie services also use free, unscrambled teasers to lure viewers to order the entire movie. If you leave your child alone in the room while you're working on a business deal or taking a swim in the pool, he may be viewing explicit sex acts in teasers ads—with the compliments of your hotel management.

The Internet

The Internet is a marvel of the twentieth century, an amazing educational tool that has connected the entire world. It gives every person who owns or otherwise has access to a computer the ability to obtain information on a scale never before imagined. While television long held the distinction of being the premier communication tool in history, it is quickly being edged out by the

Internet. Why? Because it provides endless choices to the user. With millions of Internet users on the planet, each one now has the ability to construct his or her own Web site and have an equal voice in communicating to the world. A reporter such as Matt Drudge, who operates out of an office in Miami, can compete on an equal footing with NBC, CBS, ABC, and Fox in the rapid dissemination of news.

In fact, one benefit of the Internet is that for the first time in many years, political conservatives, evangelical Christians, and other "politically incorrect" individuals can communicate to the world without being filtered by liberal news sources. No longer do we find ourselves restricted by the liberal media gatekeepers who have long refused to allow conservative or evangelical viewpoints to be heard.

Along with its benefits, however, the Internet also has its dark side. Pornographers, Planned Parenthood, and other purveyors of sexual immorality are using the Net to spread their ideas. The pornographers see your child as a potential consumer of pornographic materials, and they know that if they can get your child hooked, he or she may well become a lifelong customer. With annual worldwide pornography profits estimated to be $56 billion, it doesn't take a rocket scientist to understand that this is a lucrative business.

While pornography is mainly about greed, money, and lust, it's also about an immoral and anti-Christian philosophy that can determine the direction your child will take in life. As we saw in the preceding chapter, porn changes the brain chemistry of the user, and the person who constantly feeds this addiction can end up with serious problems. He can also become a threat to others as he begins to act out his uncontrollable sexual desires.

The Internet is probably the most dangerous threat to your children. Why? Because if your home is online, your child has instant access to the most perverted materials imaginable—bestiality; transgenders, or "she/males" (men and women who are undergoing sex-change operations); homosexuality; pedophilia; and other forms of sexual perversion. Also available are "voyeur" sites featuring college co-eds who set up video cameras in their showers and bedrooms so porn addicts can view them from the privacy of their own homes. With all that just a mouse click or two away, children can become sexually addicted far faster today than they could in the days before the Internet.

The Chat Room/Forum Threat

A chat room is a place on the Web where people can discuss their interests with others in "real time." In real time, you communicate instantly with other people. It's like being on the phone, but you're using the keyboard to communicate instead of a handset. There can be dozens of people in one chat room, carrying on a conversation.

Thousands of these chat rooms exist, and many are devoted to discussions of perverted sex. Women are increasingly getting involved in affairs with men they meet in these electronic rooms. In one recent case, a number of women were allegedly lured to their deaths by a man they met in sadomasochistic chat rooms. Pedophiles also lurk in these rooms, as well as young male predators who enjoy engaging in cybersex or actually seducing girls online.

The same threat exists in Internet forums. These are areas where individuals can post notes to each other. It isn't done in real time as in a chat room, but people can communicate rapidly by posting messages back and forth.

Relatives, Friends, Sons, Brothers, Fathers

Sadly, the danger to children from pornography isn't just from sources "out there," outside the home. As we saw in the brief story that opened this chapter, it often comes from within one's own family or circle of friends and relatives. While a vigilant mother is doing everything she can to protect her child from pornography on the Internet or in the mass media, family members or friends may be harboring a secret addiction that threatens the safety of her son or daughter.

AN UNEXPECTED PLACE

As we've seen, porn is widely and easily available today, in many different forms. But that's not the whole story. Of all the places where it can be found, one of the most common is also one that you might least expect: your neighborhood public school. This threat is widespread and serious enough that we've made it the subject of our next chapter.

CHAPTER THREE

Pornography in the Public Schools

❦

Pornography isn't found only in magazines, videos, Web sites, and phone services. Porn also includes spoken and written descriptions of sexually explicit acts, both of which your child may be exposed to in your local public school. In fact, you'll find that much of the sex education taught in schools today is pornographic in content, totally inappropriate, and without a moral framework. Some of it is openly anti-parent and anti-Christian.

Here are three more examples, among many we could cite, of what parents have encountered:

♦ In March 1997, officials at a Centreville, Virginia, elementary school assured the parents of an 11-year-old girl that she would only be exposed to a female sex-education film in her class. Instead, she was subjected to a film geared to preteen boys. It included discussions of erections, ejaculation, and wet dreams.

◆ In 1996, high school students in Chelmsford, Massachusetts, saw a sex talk and drama performance by Suzi Landolph, who conducts "Hot, Sexy and Safer" discussions. Her drama included simulated masturbation, crude language, and condom licking. Parents were not given advance notice of her performance and had no chance to opt their children out of it.

◆ In August 2000, a sixth-grade teacher on Prince Edward Island gave her 11-year-old boys and girls a detailed description of oral sex, noting that it could be done either by homosexuals or heterosexuals. The instruction took place during a four-day session covering hygiene, basic reproduction, and puberty.

We could go on for pages describing various outrages being perpetrated against children in our public schools under the guise of sex education, AIDS training, tolerance and diversity classes, and so on. *But the point is that your child may be exposed to pornographic films and explicit sexual discussions and "dramas" as part of a deliberate assault on his or her innocence.* This assault comes from Planned Parenthood and like-minded groups promoting traditional-values-free sex for teens, and from gay rights activists who are establishing Gay-Straight Alliance (GSA) clubs on junior high and high school campuses to promote the idea that homosexual conduct is a normal, acceptable alternative to heterosexuality.

As a parent, you need to understand that in modern public education, especially (but not exclusively) in the area of sex education, a philosophy of pornography prevails. The mind-set is that even young children should be exposed to explicit materials and discussions, with tolerance being expressed toward any kind of sexual activity between any two or more consenting individuals.

Much of the teaching done in sex ed classes is designed to break down the natural inhibitions of children toward sexual matters. Such teaching *desensitizes* them to sex talk. It also teaches them that intercourse and other forms of sexual contact are all normal—just varieties of sexual expression. No sense of morality is attached to premarital sex, oral sex, homosexuality, and so on. In fact, to oppose any kind of sexual activity is to be considered intolerant.

This approach to sexual matters arises from two primary sources. First is the general decline of sexual morality in Western culture, the now-widespread acceptance of extramarital sex in various forms. Second is the fact that much of the sex education material used—and the philosophy behind it—comes from groups that advocate promiscuity. Chief among these are Planned Parenthood and the Sex Information and Education Council of the United States (SIECUS).

Both of these groups have a radical agenda that is designed to stimulate an obsession with sexual activities. Planned Parenthood, a longtime supporter of abortion on demand, promotes what it calls "sexuality education," which is *nonjudgmental* and *explicit*. It has launched an attack against abstinence education, which it labels "fear-based education." SIECUS is firmly committed to promoting unrestrained sexual activities for children. In its

Events in One State

To give you a better understanding of what is becoming increasingly common in public schools, we have listed below a series of recent events in just one state, Massachusetts, as reported by Brian Camenker, president of that state's Parents' Rights Coalition, on the group's Web site in March 2001:

1. In Brookline, a transsexual adult came into a first-grade class and described to the children how sex changes take place. Parents had not been notified and had to counsel their frightened, confused children.

2. In many high schools across Massachusetts, entire days have been devoted to "Gay/Lesbian and Transgender" programs. Academic classes are cancelled and students are led to the activities, including panels, speakers, etc.

3. In Natick, high school students in the "gay-straight alliance" club were shown an R-rated movie about a graphic "love story" between two boys.

4. In Newton, school officials announced in the local newspapers that masturbation would be covered in the required courses for ninth graders.

5. At a required school assembly in Chelmsford, an instructor used four-letter words to describe the joys of oral and anal sex. Children participated in licking condoms.

6. A 14-year-old girl came home from Beverly High School and told her father that he was a "homophobe." She had just returned from "Homophobia Week" sessions at the school.

7. In schools across the state, students were told to answer surveys on their use of drugs and about personal feelings on suicide, death, homosexual activity and similar subjects. The wording was very intrusive. Parents were outraged when they found out.

8. In several towns, ninth-grade girls in the health classes were assigned to go to a drugstore, buy condoms, and practice putting them on a banana.

9. At Lexington High School, a parent discovered that her 13-year-olds could borrow a book (bought with state health funds) telling how gay men at the opera can socialize with "the backs of their trousers discreetly parted so they could experience a little extra pleasure while viewing the spectacle on stage."

10. In Newton, a high school principal told a group of parents that they may not remove their children from the condom distribution program because "it is too important."

11. At Silver Lake High School, the ninth-grade health text teaches: "Testing your ability to function sexually and to give pleasure to another person may be less threatening in the early teens with people of your own sex." Also, "You may come to the conclusion that growing-up means rejecting the values of your parents." Students were told to keep the book in their lockers and not take it home.

12. In Ashland, children were assigned to play "gays" in a school skit. One boy's line was, "It's natural to be attracted to the same sex." Two girls were told to hold hands and pretend they were lesbians. Parents were not informed.

13. In Manomet, an eighth-grade health class was given material which one boy said was against his parents' beliefs. He was told by the instructor, "If you have any trouble with your parents, tell me and I'll handle them."

14. In Nutting Lake, "counselors" conducted a group session where a girl was asked to share the details about her parents' divorce and her father's affair with the class. The sessions were to be kept confidential from parents.[1]

publication "Girls and Sex," this group says, "Sex play with boys ... can be exciting, pleasurable, and even worthwhile ... it will help later sexual adjustment."

Going along with those two groups are others like the Gay, Lesbian and Straight Education Network (GLSEN), which promote AIDS- and tolerance-education classes. These frequently include explicit discussions about homosexual sex.

A simple search of the Web sites of these groups will give you a clear idea of their ideology, their view of parents, and their goals for *your* child. These groups typically have a very negative view of parents—especially Christian parents—who wish to keep their children from being exposed to inappropriate sexual materials. In the minds of the leaders of Planned Parenthood, SIECUS, and GLSEN, *no sexual topic, discussion, or sex act is taboo for your child.*

THE KINSEY LEGACY

At the root of this modern view of sex education, and of sex in society generally, is the work of Dr. Alfred Kinsey. Kinsey was a zoologist who conducted sex experiments back in the 1940s involving pedophiles, prisoners, and children. He was also a homosexual pedophile (a pederast) who eventually published two major books that changed our culture forever: *Sexual Behavior in the Human Male* (1948) and *Sexual Behavior in the Human Female* (1953).

Kinsey concluded that there is no such thing as abnormal or deviant sexual behavior. All sexual behaviors are natural expressions of human sexuality, including homosexuality and even bestiality. Moreover, Kinsey promoted the belief that children are sexual beings from birth and should be exposed to sexual images early and often.

Since he was a pedophile, it's not surprising that he reached such conclusions and promoted such ideas. But despite his obvious bias, his work eventually gained wide acceptance.

Kinsey's writings inspired Hugh Hefner to begin *Playboy* magazine and helped launch SIECUS, the Kinsey Institute, and numerous other sexology organizations. His views are at the root of Planned Parenthood's pro-abortion and free-sex views. His faulty statistics on the prevalence of homosexuality—making it seem more common than it really is—helped propel the gay rights movement into prominence and overturn laws against sodomy. His theories on sexual behavior have become the foundation of humanistic sex education programs around the world. His writings have helped reduce penalties against rape in many states. In addition, his fraudulent work has inspired pedophiles to become militant in their efforts to normalize sex with children.

Exposing Kinsey

Make no mistake about it: Kinsey (who died in 1956) and those who have followed in his wake are promoting a sexual agenda that is antibiblical in the extreme. For greater detail about this, we suggest you read two books by Dr. Judith Reisman, who has done some of the most important work to date on the Kinsey sex philosophy. *Kinsey, Sex and Fraud,* published in 1990, exposed Kinsey's radical sexual agenda. Her more recent book *Kinsey: Crimes & Consequences* goes into greater detail about Dr. Kinsey, his associates, and their impact on sexuality and children. These books will open your eyes to what's happening in your own school district as you face a SIECUS- or Planned Parenthood-promoted sex education program.

To give you just a brief glimpse of the agenda of Kinsey's followers, consider the work of Wardell Pomeroy, a Kinsey research associate. As Dr. Reisman points out, Pomeroy has written numerous books on sex, including *Girls and Sex* and *Boys and Sex.* Both of these are recommended reading in sex education programs promoted by Planned Parenthood and SIECUS. In *Boys and Sex,* Pomeroy wrote about the positive experiences a boy can have by engaging in sex with dogs, horses, bulls, and other species.

Pomeroy has also served as a *Penthouse Forum* magazine board member. This magazine promotes incest, pedophilia, prostitution, and other forms of deviant sex as "normal." Moreover, Pomeroy has chaired a sex educator's accrediting group called the Institute for the Advanced Study of Human Sexuality. This organization awards "sexology" degrees to individuals completing their required course work. Many of these sexologists then teach in colleges and produce sex education materials for public schools.

Another sexologist cited by Dr. Reisman as having connections to the pornography industry, pedophilia, and sex education is Dr. John Money, a professor emeritus from Johns Hopkins University. At this prestigious school, Money introduced pornography as "therapy" for sexually dysfunctional individuals back in the 1960s. His presentation, called "Pornography in the Home," has been used at Johns Hopkins Medical School. Several years ago, Money gave an interview to the pro-pedophile *Paidika: The Journal of Paedophilia.* In it, Money said he could see nothing wrong with consensual adult/child sex. This sexologist is still quoted frequently in the mainstream press about sexual issues.

What the Philosophy of Pornography Has Done to Our Culture

Here are a just a couple more examples of how Kinsey's philosophy of pornography has infected the public school system:

◆ In March 2000, GLSEN held a "Teach Out" at Tufts University in Boston for school teachers and teenagers. At this conference, several state-employed HIV instructors (lesbians and gay men) conducted workshops on how to fight "homophobia" and the "religious right" in the public schools; how to introduce homosexual themes into history lessons; and how to engage in homosexual sex acts. In one graphic workshop, the three HIV instructors taught teens how to "fist" their sexual partners. (Fisting is a practice where a person shoves his arm up the rectum of his partner.) The leaders also explained that it's okay to swallow male body fluids during oral sex. In addition, they said that teens could make an informed "choice" *not* to use condoms during anal intercourse. This workshop and several more were caught on tape by a representative of the pro-family Parents Rights Coalition, a Massachusetts-based group. The description we have just given is tame compared to what was actually said by the homosexual instructors at this conference.

♦ In June 2000, the New Milford (Connecticut) board of education was threatened with a class action lawsuit by parents outraged over an explicit sex survey conducted of their 11-year-old children. The survey, administered to 400 children, asked if these kids had ever engaged in oral sex or had ever used drugs or alcohol before engaging in sexual intercourse. While the school claimed it sent home a permission slip with each child for a parent to sign, many parents said they never received it.

GETTING INVOLVED

Suffice it to say that parents cannot just assume that all is well at their child's public school. If you haven't already done so, you need to investigate your school's sex education and AIDS/diversity/tolerance teaching materials. In addition, you need to realize that the teaching of English, sociology, and other subjects has also been influenced. Sexually explicit themes are fre-

quently introduced in history classes. A lesbian elementary school teacher who taught a GLSEN workshop
at Tufts bragged about how she had introduced homosexuality into her lesson on the Nazi Holocaust. She
encouraged other teachers to use the same technique to
indoctrinate children into accepting homosexuality as
normal.

To protect your child against that kind of teaching,
take time to talk with him regularly about what he's
hearing in school. Let him know you want to be
informed about any discussions of sexual matters or the
showing of films with sexual content in any class. Monitor what kind of essays he's being asked to write. Assure
him that you'll defend him if he's subjected to discussions that make him feel uncomfortable. Help him
understand that you're allies in this, not adversaries.

To help you evaluate the sex education program at
your child's school, Focus on the Family's CitizenLink
Web site provides a checklist you can use. We reprint it
here for your convenience, but we urge you to regularly
visit CitizenLink for updates on this topic and others
(www.fotf.org/cforum).

Evaluating Your School District's
Sex Education Program

From CitizenLink

Nobody cares about your child more than you do.
Therefore, you, as a parent, have the most important
role in the education of your child, and that is to
make sure that he is being educated well and

responsibly. One of the areas where this responsibility is most significant is in the area of sexuality education. With the rampant spread of adolescent pregnancy and sexually transmitted diseases (STDs), more schools are making the discussion of human sexuality a part of their curriculum. The trouble is that instruction on such an issue can be very volatile. Some of the curricula can be very helpful and educational, while others can be nothing more than the introduction of alternative sexual values that have very unhealthy consequences for your child. How can you distinguish one from the other?

SUBJECT AREAS

Parents should evaluate a variety of areas when examining their school's sex education materials. They should gather information about how the material deals with the following areas:

- ◆ Role of Parent in the School's Decision-making Process
- ◆ Portrayal of Parent in the Curriculum
- ◆ Moral Perspective
- ◆ Sexual Development
- ◆ View Toward Abstinence
- ◆ Consequences of Promiscuity
- ◆ Sexually Transmitted Diseases
- ◆ Alternative Lifestyles
- ◆ Contraception

- Adoption
- Character & Social Development
- Marriage
- Family
- Human Reproduction
- Parenting

PARTICIPATION IN THE PROCESS

Beyond reviewing the actual materials your child will be using in class, you may want to participate in a number of different areas:

1. Ask the school if you can participate in the teacher training classes that will be held if a proposed sex education curriculum is accepted. Often, the philosophy and "spirit" of the course are conveyed by the leaders who conduct the teacher training sessions.

2. Commit to serving on sex education committees. Get a commitment from your school that sex ed committees and task forces will reflect a majority of parents rather than special interest groups....

3. Attend meetings with suggestions of possible curricula, [along with] studies and supplemental materials that support your views and desires for the sex education program.

4. Challenge your committee to give parents as many choices for their child as possible in this most sensitive subject.

What to Do When You Have a Concern

If you discover at any time that your child is being exposed to pornographic movies, inappropriate sex education materials, pro-homosexual recruitment programs, or anything else objectionable, follow the suggestions given below by Dr. Perry Glanzer in a CitizenLink article:

> When parents face a possible rights violation, they should use a ladder approach: Start with the teacher or school official who teaches or directs the class or program, and work up the "ladder" of authority. If the teacher or official is approached courteously and respectfully, and the parents assume that the teacher or official wants to act in the best interests of the class and their child, they are likely to have less trouble when trying to clear up the matter.
>
> 1. When communicating with any school authority, parents should make it clear that they want to work with the authority and that their concerns are not personal. In addition, they should express their concerns as specifically as possible.... Parents should also find out the teacher or official's reasons for using the material or requiring the program. Often, a substitute can be found which provides the information or activity that fits the educational goal and addresses parental concerns.

If there is no other material or alternative program that fulfills the goal of the lesson, parents should request that their child be excused or an alternative assignment given to their child. They may even want to request that their child be assigned to another class.

Making a Positive Impact

Involvement with your child's school should not happen only when you have a cause for concern or something negative to say. There are many ways to make a regular, positive impact and affirm the good things the teacher and staff are doing. One in particular that you might consider is to support the responsible use of technology.

Here are some ways in which you could do that:

♦ Ask your local PTA to set up a "family night" on computers, technology, and the Internet.

♦ If the school can't afford computer hardware for students, help obtain used equipment from government agencies or businesses. For information on computer recycling, visit www.microweb.com/pepsite/Recycle/recycle_index. html.

♦ Organize a training session for teachers and other parents, perhaps recruiting a volunteer instructor from a local computer retailer.

♦ If you have technology expertise yourself, volunteer in your child's class or computer lab.

♦ Offer to help the school develop and implement a responsible Internet use policy and software solutions to ensure that students' Web access is safe and educational.

♦ If the school has a technology planning group, volunteer to serve in it.[2]

2. If the teacher refuses to accommodate the parents, they should then meet with the principal. Often it is helpful to find other parents who may share their concern.

3. If the principal shows no sensitivity to their complaint, parents should consider meeting with a member of the school board who would be most receptive to their concern and would be willing to discuss their complaint. At this point, parents should be aware of their legal rights in the area of concern. Contact your state board of education with specific questions (e.g., "What is our state law regarding excusal from sex-education programs?"). Often individual meetings with school board members will further communication and prevent miscommunication in the event that a larger public debate at a school board meeting is required.

4. If these steps do not lead to a satisfactory solution, parents should attend a school board meeting and share their concerns during the public comment time. If the school administration does not respond, parents can take their case to the local media such as newspapers, magazines, and television and radio stations.

5. When the school teachers, principal and school board are unwilling to deal with the parents' concern, the parents may want to consider other educational options for their children such as enrolling them in a private school or teaching them at home.

Knowing Your Rights

Before you approach a teacher or school official with your concerns, it's also important for you to know your rights as a parent. Just what they are will depend on what laws exist in your state and how they're implemented in your particular school district. Laws change frequently, so you'll have to do your homework to confirm what rights you have at any given time. A local chapter of the American Family Association, Eagle Forum, or Concerned Women for America may have current information. Log on to their Web sites for local resource information.

Whatever the laws in your community, there are certain rights that every parent *should* have. The following list includes rights that many states have adopted. Ideally, you should have the right:

♦ to see instructional materials used in research programs funded by the Department of Education and National Science Foundation. (Many of these programs include explicit sexual materials.)

♦ to visit your child's classroom at any time during the day, providing you first notify the school office.

♦ to exclude your child from studying subjects you object to on religious, moral, or other reasonable grounds.

♦ to have your child excluded from reading objectionable books on religious, moral, or other reasonable grounds.

♦ to have your child excused from objectionable school activities.

♦ to look at all your child's records and challenge any record you believe is unfair.

♦ to look at all school policies.

♦ to appeal a school policy that prevents your child from expressing a controversial view.

♦ to speak at all public meetings of the local school board.

♦ to attend all meetings of the school board (except for executive sessions).

♦ to appeal school board decisions to a higher authority.

♦ to be a member of any parent/citizen group and have your group recognized and heard by school officials.

♦ to appeal the suspension of your child.

The Context

As you pursue your parental rights, it also helps to bear in mind the cultural context in which any discussion with school officials will take place. Focus on the Family's CitizenLink Web site again provides helpful information. Below are portions of an article titled "Parental Rights in Public Education" and written, again, by Dr. Perry Glanzer:

> Clinton caused a stir when she used the proverb, "It takes a village to raise a child," as a basis for her book title. At one level, the proverb captures a truth we all recognize: No family is an island. Parents often want and need assistance in the

upbringing and education of their children. They may eagerly seek assistance from their local "village" of family, friends, and neighbors. Furthermore, they are likely to accept the supportive help of intermediary village institutions such as the church, youth clubs, or other voluntary associations. Yet, the problem is that this nice-sounding phrase fails to guide us through the labyrinth of complex issues that arise when the *government* village attempts to help parents raise their children. These issues become especially problematic when the government village is a public school with political power.

For example, two Georgia parents recently received a "helping hand" from the school village that they did not know about or appreciate. During school hours, a counselor drove their 13- and 15-year-old daughters to a county health clinic where they received Pap smears, AIDS tests, condoms, and birth-control pills. The parents were not informed in advance about the trip or the medical procedures. When the parents contacted the school district and the county health clinic for results of the tests, the parents were told, "It's none of your business" because of patient confidentiality.

In another instance, one California couple learned about the "help" their school village was offering and found out that they were not permitted to reject the help. As Christians, they wanted to teach their kids about dating, drinking, and values themselves. When they found that a class at the high school called "Decision Making" was teaching their son sex education, sexual orientation, stress and death management, values clarification, and other nonacademic subjects, they asked that their son be excused from the class. The sex education portion, according to California law, was already optional. However, the school district refused to allow their boy to be dismissed from the other portions of the class, because this non-academic course was required for graduation. The conflict was discussed in two different newspaper articles. One editorial claimed that educators and elected school board members, not parents, should decide whether the "Decision Making" class would be optional. Another columnist noted the irony of this approach and commented, "The district says it wants to teach decision-making to kids, but won't allow it to their parents." ...

These cases reveal the fierce battle over the roles of parents and schools in directing the upbringing and education of children. Who is the ultimate authority in a child's life? Will parents or the school village have the final word about what a child is taught? Will parents or the school village have the final word about whether children can opt in or out of a class? Will parents or the school village have the final say on when a child is considered ready to make decisions about difficult areas of life?

The unavoidable fact is that today, many school officials and judges fail to remember that "the child is not the mere creature of the state." They forget that children are gifts from God and that He has given parents the responsibility to direct the upbringing and education of their children. Consequently, employees of the school village may seek to take this responsibility from parents. Such is the society in which we live.

DR. REISMAN ADVISES PARENTS

As noted earlier, Dr. Judith Reisman has done significant research exposing the radical agenda of groups that embrace the conclusions and philosophy of Alfred Kinsey. In her writings, she encourages parents to take an aggressive, proactive approach to keeping those groups out of their children's schools. In an article titled "Sex Educators as Arsonists on the Fire Brigade Merry-Go-Round," she wrote, "According to existing law in most states, schools and/or teachers that present sexual/erotic heterosexual or homosexual 'information' in any form are criminally liable, engaged in sexual misconduct for contributing to the delinquency of minors, exposing minors to 'harmful matter.'

"School board members, superintendents, principals and others involved in the selection of administrators, teachers, coaches, counselors, lecturers, presenters, or in selecting sexual/erotic media for any government, private or parochial or home school system should be similarly put on notice of criminal liability in the distribution of 'harmful matter.'

"Responsible officials and parents need to come in out of the politically correct fog. Children are truly at-risk. A statement should be signed by you [the parent] and/or your organization and sent via certified mail to authorities in your school system and members of your state legislature, calling for the elimination of all funds allotted to any programs based on Kinsey's 'work' or that of his disciples in the sexology field such as SIECUS and Planned Parenthood.

"These groups—which have been searing school children with incinerating sexual/erotic material justified by Kinsey's fraudulent research—should be immediately defunded."[3]

WHEN ALL ELSE FAILS

Finally, if all attempts to work out concerns with school officials have failed, and an alternative education is not an option for your child for whatever reason, you may have to consider obtaining legal assistance. Even at this stage, however, it's best to act prudently. A letter from a law firm is often helpful, since school officials may not be familiar with the law and related case precedents. Groups that specialize in defending the rights of parents in public education can be helpful. While these legal groups may not take your case, they might be able to offer advice and referrals.

If you fail to get cooperation from school officials, you may have to think about filing a lawsuit. Grounds for the suit might be violations of your state's "harmful to minors statute" (if one is in place). In addition, teachers who promote homosexuality may be violating your state's prohibition against sodomy. Fewer than half the states still have laws against sodomy, but if your state is one that does, you can file charges against teachers who encourage children to break the law. Teachers who openly promote sex between minors and/or adults may also be violating your state's "age of consent" laws. These laws proscribe minors from engaging in sex with one another or with adults.

We'll list some law firms and organizations in the resource appendix that may be able to help if you need legal assistance. Regrettably, a threatened lawsuit is often the only way to get public school officials to do the right thing.

Even legal recourse may fail if strong laws protecting parental rights in education do not exist. Therefore, you may need to work to pass legislation or school-district policies that would protect parental rights. In addition, you might consider running for your school board. That way, win or lose, you would have a forum for promoting parent-friendly policies.

In a famous quotation, we are told that "the condition upon which God hath given liberty to man is eternal vigilance." Sadly, in this day and age, parents must also keep constant, prayerful vigilance over what their children are being shown and taught in public schools.

Otherwise, those kids are liable to be exposed to pornography of one or more kinds right there in the classroom.

The good news, however, is that conscientious parents *can* protect their children. There's no need to despair, only a need to stay informed and involved.

CHAPTER FOUR

Parents, Are You Creating or Allowing a Problem?

Kurt Stansell admits that he's a sex addict. He has gone to X-rated theaters and strip clubs, watched pornographic movies at home and in his hotel room while on business trips, and looked through countless magazines. He fought the addiction for years on his own, sometimes succeeding for months at a time before eventually succumbing to temptation once again.

How did Kurt's struggles all get started? Like every adolescent, he developed a normal interest in sex. He got his first exposure to pornography, which further fueled his fantasies. And then he adds tellingly that for some reason, "my dad wasn't there for me at that point."[1]

His dad didn't do anything terribly overtly wrong, like taking his teenage son to a men's club. But by allowing an emotional distance to grow between them at a critical time in his son's development, he left questions unanswered, fears unspoken, and anxieties unexpressed. And so, in secret, Kurt's natural curiosity took a wrong turn toward unhealthy, sinful obsession.

As that simple story of an all-too-common experience shows, we parents have a powerful impact, for good or ill, on our children's development—often without realizing just what that impact is. What we say and do—or don't say and don't do—will largely determine whether they're equipped to succeed or fail at dealing with the X-ratedness of our culture.

Dangerous Family Patterns

Psychologist Rob Jackson, who has treated hundreds of sex addicts, has identified a number of common family patterns that can set up a child for addiction or at least confusion about his sexuality or relationships with the opposite sex. These patterns have to do with the attitudes within a family—its spiritual and emotional "climate"—not the family structure itself.

Here are the dangerous patterns:

♦ *A home that has loose boundaries on sexual matters*. A family with loose sexual boundaries is one in which little modesty is displayed. Mom and Dad may walk around the house in their underwear in full view of the children. Or a parent may invade the privacy of a child who is in the bathroom, taking a shower or even using the toilet. There may be inappropriate sex talk as well. Parents may allow their kids to watch sexually stimulating material on TV, at the movies, or on the Internet. The children may be allowed to have sexually enticing posters or CDs in their rooms.

◆ *A home with overly rigid sexual boundaries.* In this home, a child is either told that sex is evil or is denied any information about it at all. As a result, he thinks that he is evil or perverted when he begins to have sexual thoughts and desires. He may also start to obsess over sex because it's "forbidden fruit." He will search for information about sex from his peers, MTV, movies, the Internet, or other inappropriate sources.

◆ *A home filled with anger.* In a home filled with anger, one parent may be exploding with verbal abuse or even physical violence. The other may be imploding with anger, repressing her true feelings. An angry home is one where injustice rules because there are confusing guidelines about what is good and bad behavior. What may have been "right" one day will be "wrong" the next, leaving a child emotionally unbalanced and fearful. This hostile environment will deeply wound a child's spirit, causing him to "self-medicate" and seek comfort in pleasure wherever he can find it. The child is attempting to meet a legitimate need for peace and security, but he may do so in destructive ways. Pornography, for example, provides good feelings and "unconditional acceptance" from the women he is viewing. He may eventually go deeper and deeper into a full-blown sexual addiction. If that happens, he might learn to avoid real relationships and prefer to live in a fantasy world where no one judges him or has any expectations of him.

◆ *A home where one parent is the abandoner and the other is the enmesher.* In this family dynamic, one parent is emotionally distant and unavailable to the child (like Kurt Stansell's dad). The other parent, the enmesher, gets too close to her child and smothers him. The parent who overnurtures creates what Jackson calls emotional incest. The child feels betrayed by one parent and stifled by the other. Dr. Harry Schaumburg, writing in *False Intimacy: Understanding the Struggle of Sexual Addiction,* pointed out that children in homes like this feel lonely, abandoned, and filled with self-doubt. In their search for love and stability, they frequently discover a counterfeit by pursuing pornographic images that are always available at the click of a mouse, on the scrambled Playboy network, in the magazine hidden under the bed, or in the video smuggled into the home.

◆ *A home where one parent is authoritarian and the other is passive.* In this home, one parent makes all the decisions. The other parent is without power, and so are the children. In a home where the authoritarian is cruel, a child feels unsafe, unloved, and a victim of unreasonable rules. This is a breeding ground for bitterness and rebellion. A child may seek safety in the world of pornography, where there are no rules, no parents, no consequences, and total freedom to do whatever one can fantasize.

♦ *A home where both parents work and the children are unsupervised for long periods of time.* Children with uncontrolled access to TV, videos, and the Internet will frequently succumb to the temptation to view inappropriate materials. They will also be influenced by friends who may have pornographic magazines, computer diskettes, or videos to trade.

♦ *A home where there is lack of respect for the children.* Kids should be taught to respect their parents and other adults, but parents should also respect their children as human beings with feelings who have the need for approval and love. If there's a lack of mutual love or respect in the home, a child will seek it elsewhere, perhaps by turning to drugs, alcohol, promiscuous sex, pornography, or even crime. All these things will provide a false sense of self-esteem, fulfillment, and control over his life.

♦ *A home where one or both parents are involved in pornography themselves.* A child often becomes involved in pornography when he discovers his father's hidden stash of magazines or videos. Kids are curious by nature. They rummage through drawers, cabinets, under beds, and so on just because they're eager to explore. If there is pornography in the house, children will eventually discover it.

In Rob Jackson's experience, these are typical family dynamics that set up a child to begin searching for sexual materials. The child is looking for security, love, and approval, and that search goes off in the wrong direction. In such cases, the entire family needs to be helped.

INTERNAL MOTIVATIONS TOWARD
A SEX ADDICTION

The kinds of family dynamics just described produce ʻ internal motivations for a child to seek pornographic materials. Dr. Harry W. Schaumburg, in *False Intimacy,* has expanded on a few of these. According to Schaumburg, a child who is vulnerable to a sex addiction is experiencing the following feelings:

♦ *Fear of intimacy:* When parents fail to touch, nurture, and express genuine love for their children, the kids learn to fear intimacy. Likewise, if a child's affection is routinely rejected by a parent, or if a parent is untrustworthy, the child will either shut down emotionally or seek intimacy in other ways. In addition, a child who is subjected to sexual abuse is certainly going to fear intimacy.

♦ *Feelings of abandonment:* Parental conflict, anger, frequent separations, and the potential for divorce will create a child who fears being abandoned. So will living in a home where one or both parents are emotionally absent.

♦ *Lack of appreciation:* When both parents are working or are caught up in their own needs and desires, a child will frequently feel starved for appreciation. Such a child will seek appreciation elsewhere.

♦ *Loneliness:* Children can feel alone in their families if parents fail to talk, listen, pray, and play with them. And if they're lonely, they will seek companionship of one kind or another.

These feelings won't necessarily lead a child into a pornography addiction, but they can. They're certainly risk factors that every parent should be aware of. Schaumburg suggests that parents make sure their

---

Retreat into Porn

[Kevin's] home looked ideal. He grew up with two loving parents who made family a priority. What could be better? But Kevin's father disliked confrontation and conflict and gladly relinquished discipline of the children to his wife. During Kevin's first seven years, his dad traveled as a salesman three weeks out of every four, and, when he was home, disappeared to the bedroom at the first sign of any trouble.

Forced to function almost like a single parent, Kevin's mother used the only tools she was familiar with to ensure Kevin's and his sister's obedience—shame and guilt, yelling and threatening. When Kevin was four, he wet his pants. He couldn't remember the events that led to his accident, but he will never forget how his mother handled the situation. She diapered him and forced him out the door while he screamed and cried. Kevin had to endure the jeering of the other children in their apartment complex, as they laughed to see a four-year-old in "baby diapers." That was the first day he felt shameful....

His mother's shaming techniques and his father's avoidance led Kevin to a place of painful self-isolation. He became adept at showing everyone his "good" side, and determined he would have to learn to solve his own problems in private. In his "secret life," like many kids, he tried alcohol and cigarettes; but ... when he was ten, he discovered the "medication" that had drawn his father to retreat to his bedroom at the first sign of conflict—pornography.[2]

home is one where children can express their desires and concerns in a safe environment. Children must know that they are loved by their parents and that they can freely reveal their sexual struggles and temptations without fear of being condemned or accused of being a pervert.

If your child is lonely, feeling unappreciated or unloved, or fears he will be abandoned, you're not going to know unless you ask him!

Is he sexually confused? Again, the only way you will find out is by open, loving, and nonjudgmental communication.

Is he sexually ignorant? It's your job to make sure he has accurate information about sexuality from a biblical perspective.

Is he seeing you and your spouse modeling a godly relationship between a man and a woman in marriage? Whether you realize it or not, you're teaching your child every day about sexuality, God, integrity, relationships, and more. Your actions speak far louder than your words.

WOMEN: IF YOUR HUSBAND IS USING PORNOGRAPHY

What should a wife do if she discovers her husband is using pornography? H. B. London Jr., the vice president of pastoral ministries at Focus on the Family, gives the following advice on Focus's "Parsonage.com" Web site:

◆ **Remember it is not about you.** You (the wife) are not to blame, nor should you carry shame. Don't allow your spouse to lay false guilt on you.

◆ **Establish boundaries.** Your husband needs help. You must draw a line so that his behavior is not perceived as acceptable. It may demand tough love.

◆ **Find a support network.** You should find a friend, pastor, mentor, support group, or counselor who can provide you with insight and advice. (EstherOnline.org is a women's ministry devoted to helping wives deal with their husbands' addiction. You may wish to consult this Web site for advice and contacts.)

◆ **Support your spouse's recovery.** He needs someone like you to hold him accountable. Keep the lines of communication open. Pray with him about his problem.

◆ **Do not ignore any recurrence of the behavior.** Carefully confront your husband about any changes that indicate he is returning to his previous sinful habit.

This advice is based on your husband's willingness to get help. But what action can you take when he refuses to listen? In *False Intimacy*, Dr. Schaumburg suggests you arrange for an "intervention." This will involve a meeting between you, a counselor or respected friend, and your husband, forcing him to confront his sexual sin and the harm it's doing to him, your marriage (through, e.g., the Centerfold Syndrome and his lack of trustworthiness), and your children.

If your intervention fails to change your husband's heart and mind, consider alerting your pastor to your husband's problem and enlisting his help. You should also remove the pornographic materials from your home. This is going to cause conflict, so be ready for it. You have an obligation to protect your children from these materials even if it upsets your husband.

If you discover your husband has gone beyond using porn to having sex with other women, he is putting you at risk for sexually transmitted diseases or AIDS infection, and you should consider ending all sexual relations with him.

If you discover that he has been acting out sexually with your children or any others, you must strongly consider contacting the police. Once he has reached this point, he is out of control and has become a threat to others. If you're facing this situation, it may be wise to separate from your husband for your own safety and that of your children.

Fortunately, pornography addiction can be overcome. Kurt Stansell, whose story we introduced at the beginning of this chapter, is one who eventually found freedom from his obsession. With help from a friend with whom he could be brutally honest, a compassionate pastor, and a small group of men from his church, he gradually was able to set aside the world of fantasy and build a better relationship with his wife. Said Kurt, "I've finally learned that God's instructions for us are there for a reason.... He really does want what's best for me; He's not making up the rules arbitrarily. And when we follow His plan and work for His ideal, He amazes us with His blessing and the natural consequences that follow.... My marriage now truly exceeds all the fantasies I ever had."[3]

Kurt Stansell has experienced freedom and new wholeness because he was willing to confess his sinful behavior—and his need for help. This same deliverance is available to any Christian hooked on porn.

MEN: TAKING RESPONSIBILITY

Fathers hold the key to spiritual wholeness within the family. As the Lord's appointed head, you are not only to be the financial provider but also the spiritual head. And you must be concerned for your family's physical and emotional safety as well.

Accordingly, as a father, you must make certain *you* are not engaged in any activities that could jeopardize the spiritual safety of your family. This includes avoiding any use of pornographic materials.

Many men were introduced to porn by discovering it in their home when they were kids. Because of the sinful habits of their fathers or older brothers, these men are now struggling with the same problem.

If you maintain a secret stash of pornographic materials or surf the Net looking for pornographic sites, you can be fairly sure your children will find out. Kids are curious by nature, and they frequently snoop around the house for the fun of it. Nothing hidden by a porn user will remain hidden for long. Therefore, don't think you're going to get away with living a double life.

Instead, do whatever it takes to protect yourself and your family from exposure to pornography. If you secretly view it, you are jeopardizing your wife and children's future. If you're tempted to use it, do the following:

♦ **Remove whatever influences are in your home that would give you access to pornography.** Get an Internet filtering software package or Internet service provider that blocks porn sites. Don't subscribe to cable or satellite channels that show sexually explicit materials. Don't purchase porn magazines or even a magazine featuring women in swimsuits.

♦ **Become accountable to someone or to a group.** If you're wrestling with temptation, you'll benefit greatly from the counsel and support of others who are going through the same battles. Try to locate a men's support group or a church-based group where you can honestly and confidentially make known your struggles and be held lovingly accountable.

♦ **Confess your temptations to your wife.** Confession brings secret sins into the open, where they frequently lose their power over a person. If you struggle with pornography, you should encourage your wife to hold you accountable.

♦ **Talk to your kids about the dangers of porn.** Once your struggles are in the open, make sure your kids know about the dangers of porn. They should not learn about this topic from their peers or from movies or TV. At what age should you begin? Regrettably, since children are being exposed at younger and younger ages, you may have to start discussing pornography with your five-year-old—especially if he has already been exposed.

◆ **Make certain your children are not viewing pornographic materials at a friend's house.** Get to know your children's friends and their parents' standards. If you learn that your kids are seeing forbidden materials at a friend's home, that home should become off-limits until you can discuss viewing restrictions with the parents.

One Man's Struggle

Wally, a businessman and frequent traveler, told us he absolutely dreads hotels. "I always eat a long, leisurely supper," he says, "stalling before returning to my room because I know what's coming. Before too long, I have the TV remote in my hand. I tell myself it'll only be for a minute, but I know I'm lying. I know what I really want. I'm hoping to catch a little sex scene or two as I search the channels. I tell myself that I'll only watch for a while, or that I'll stop before I get carried away. Then my motor gets going and I lust for more, sometimes even turning to the X-rated channel.

"The RPMs are going so high I have to do something, or it feels like my engine will blow. On a few occasions I fight it, but if I do, later on when I turn the lights out, I'm flooded with lustful thoughts and desires. I stare wide-eyed at the ceiling. I see nothing, but I literally feel the bombardment. I have no way to get to sleep, and it's killing me. The guilt is so strong I still can't get to sleep. I wake up totally exhausted in the morning.

"What's wrong with me? Do other men have this problem? I'm afraid to ask, really. What if this isn't how everyone else is? What would that say about me? Worse, what if this is how everyone else is? What would that say about the church?"[4]

◆ **Pray that porn will never invade your home.** The Lord doesn't want your home to be polluted by pornography or for you to become a slave to sinful habits. So pray specifically that you and your family will never come under the bondage of porn.

SPECIAL CHALLENGES FOR SINGLE PARENTS

Single parents face special challenges as they deal with pornography and their children. One great challenge is to somehow provide proper opposite-sex role models so that the kids don't feel abandoned, as discussed above. Children, especially children without at-home fathers, are at great risk for getting into all sorts of trouble.

In addition, single parents face the challenge of protecting their kids from exposure to pornographic materials without the help of a spouse. If the children need caregivers before or after school, those people may not share the parents' values. If the children are left home alone, they may get into mischief on their own.

To deal with this situation, the single parent needs to establish clear guidelines with caregivers and their children about what the kids can view on television, the Net, and the VCR or DVD player. Here are some basic guidelines to consider:

◆ The TV or VCR/DVD player will not be used as a baby-sitter.

◆ Children will be under constant supervision by their caregivers.

• Under no circumstances will children be allowed to watch PG-13 or R-rated movies—especially on cable or satellite channels. If they're allowed to watch movies at all, the parent should approve the viewing choices beforehand.

• If children are being cared for at someone else's home, they should not be given access to an unfiltered computer. Nor should they watch movies or programs or play video games that the parent has not approved.

• If children are taken by caregivers to a library, or they go there on their own to wait for parents to pick them up after work, they are not to use Internet-connected computers that aren't filtered, regardless of library rules that may be more lenient.

If your children are old enough to stay at home by themselves, take care to remove or block any media that may provide them with access to pornographic materials. If you subscribe to movie channels, use the parental control options provided by your cable or satellite service. If dial-a-porn sex could be a temptation, contact your phone company to have blocking placed on 900 numbers. You can't control what your kids bring into the house without your knowledge, but don't be afraid to ask if they're looking at videos, magazines, or other materials that are dishonoring to the Lord. Unless they have become skilled at hiding the truth, you may get a tearful confession from them.

Pray for God to give you supernatural insights into what your children are doing and what they're accessing in your home. A friend recently felt led to pray more intentionally for her teenage son. One day soon after, as she was cleaning in his room, she found three pages of pornographic pictures. She and her husband were then able to have a good discussion with their son about why it's wrong for anyone other than a woman's husband to view her nakedness.

What About the Ex-Spouse?

In the case of a divorced couple, the ex-spouse may have dramatically different values from the custodial parent's. When their child visits the ex-spouse, he or she may be exposed to things the custodial parent finds objectionable, including porn.

When that happens, the mom (still usually the custodial parent) should meet with the ex-husband to discuss ground rules for what their child can and cannot see on TV or the Internet. If they can't agree, the mom may have to go to court and ask the judge to impose proper standards on the ex-husband. A good family attorney can guide the single parent through various options.

SPECIAL CHALLENGES FOR BLENDED FAMILIES

With the breakdown of the traditional family in our culture in recent years, it's now common for families to be "blended"—to be a combination of two divorced persons and their children. Family counselor Gary Smalley notes that 79 percent of divorced men and 75 percent of divorced women remarry, usually within three to four years. An estimated 10 million children live in blended families at the time of this writing.[5]

The parents in these blended families face serious challenges in making everything work. One of the biggest involves the possibility of sexual tension in the new family. This tension can exist between the stepfather and his stepdaughters or between stepsiblings who are suddenly thrown together in the home.

According to Peter K. Gerlach, a social worker who cofounded the Stepfamily Association of Illinois, the "incest taboo" in blended families is far weaker than in traditional families. He notes a recent study suggesting that the odds of a girl under 18 being molested are four times higher with male step-relatives than with biologically related relatives. "A related family difference occurs when a man remarries a much younger new wife who is only a few years older than his oldest son or daughter," Gerlach continues. "Sexual feelings may develop between the new wife and her stepson. In other stepfamilies, if both remarrying partners have teenagers, the possibility of sexual attraction and action between the teens is significantly higher than in average bio-family homes."[6]

Given this reality, parents in a blended family with children need to be especially careful not to let pornography invade their home and corrupt the hearts and minds of family members. They also need to think carefully about making sure their new-sibling teens are given no opportunity to get into sexually compromising situations.

Another serious challenge for stepparents is the daunting task of enforcing discipline on their spouse's children. In many cases, the stepparent wishes to escape his role as disciplinarian. Gary Smalley notes that it takes about two years for a step-relationship to develop to the point where the stepparent can actually begin disciplining his nonbiological children. And this difficulty in administering discipline can be a key sticking point in setting proper guidelines for TV, movie, Internet, and other media use.

Both parents need to reach an agreement on their children's access to media, especially if it involves potential exposure to pornographic materials. They also need to jointly develop guidelines on where their children are allowed to go and who their friends will be. Then they need to be united and consistent in enforcing those rules.

If there are step-teenage girls and boys in the home, the parents must also work out privacy and modesty issues. Will nonrelated girls and boys share the same bathroom? It would be better if they used different bathrooms—preferably in different parts of the home. It would also be best if they did not wear revealing clothing in public areas of the home.

Yet another challenge for stepparents is that when two families with children are blended, they typically bring with them much pain, anger, and rebellion. As we saw earlier in this chapter, these are emotions and attitudes that often lead to a search for comfort in such unsafe areas as pornography.

Teenagers are especially prone to acting out their pain in destructive ways. Dr. Archibald Hart, writing in *Helping Children Survive Divorce*, noted, "Typically … teenagers withdraw and try emotionally to escape from the new marriage. They remain distant and refuse to be incorporated into the new family unit. The problem may be further complicated if the new spouse also brings children into the marriage."[7]

Hart urges stepparents to take an inventory of the potential problems their children are bringing into the blended marriage. Among those are:

* Patterns of behavior: violence, lying, acting jealous, territorial behavior
* Fear
* Rebellion
* Emotional problems: anger, distrust, anxiety, depression, shame

Blended Family Realities

Pornography poses a great risk to biological families. It poses an even greater challenge to blended families. The split in authority between the parents, the anger and pain experienced by the children, the upheaval caused by moving into a new home—all these issues and more can provide a volatile impetus for children to get involved in forbidden activities.

If you're moving into a blended family situation, consider getting professional counseling for you, your spouse, and the children who will be brought together. A good counselor can help everyone understand what the stresses and dangers will be. Emotional issues may also need to be uncovered and discussed; a further resource in this area is Dr. Hart's excellent book *Helping Children Survive Divorce*.

SETTING GUIDELINES

Here are a few suggested guidelines for parents who want to do all they can to keep pornography out of their homes:

• Every computer with Internet access will have a filter installed on it, or the family will subscribe to an Internet service provider that blocks pornography sites.

• You have the right to block access to questionable channels on every TV in the home.

• You have the right to screen the contents of rental movies for the VCR or DVD player.

• Children cannot order pay-per-view films without parental permission.

• If objectionable material comes on the TV, the channel is changed immediately.

• Everyone is accountable to other members of the family. When one person is engaging in conduct that would be disapproved of by the parents, the other siblings have an obligation to make this known.

• Relationships in the family will be based on honor, trust, and mutual respect. However, no child has an unrestricted right to privacy. Your kids should understand that your home is an open place, and no one has secrets. If you have reason to suspect a family member is doing something harmful, like using porn (or drugs), you have the right to search any area of the house and the hard drive of any computer.

• The Bible will be the guiding rulebook in the family, the final authority on matters of morality. In addition, members of the family will be expected to attend church and to join in family prayer and/or Bible study times. (This should be applied flexibly, however. Teens need a good youth program. If your church doesn't have one, consider going elsewhere.)

We encourage you to pray each day that your children will be shielded from actions or attitudes within the home that could predispose them to seek out pornographic materials. As Dr. James Dobson has written in *Parenting Isn't for Cowards,* "I urge you to hold your children before the Lord in fervent prayer throughout their years at home. I am convinced that there is no other source of confidence and wisdom in parenting. There is not enough knowledge in the books, mine or anyone else's, to counteract the evil that surrounds our kids today.... We must bathe them in prayer every day of their lives. The God who made your children *will* hear your petitions. He has promised to do so. After all, He loves them more than you do."[8] Amen!

CHAPTER FIVE

Preparing Our Kids Mentally and Spiritually

Imagine that your child is faced every day with an easy opportunity to view pornography. He even gets encouragement to indulge—perhaps a good friend has found his father's stash of magazines. And most tempting of all, he knows he could probably get away with it without ever being caught.

How would you want your child to respond to that temptation day after day?

No doubt you'd like him to say something like this: "How could I do such a wicked thing and sin against God?" And then you'd like him to "flee" from the pornographic material, as 2 Timothy 2:22 prescribes.

The bad news is that unless you live in a closed community without a TV or radio or friends who own them, and you never allow your child in stores that carry magazines, and you somehow cover your child's eyes every time your car approaches a billboard, and so on, it is likely that your child is going to be exposed to sex talk and even sexual images. It's unavoidable in this sex-saturated culture. The checkout stand at the grocery store alone contains sexually charged magazine covers. Though you can do a lot to shield your child, as we're explaining in this book, no parental shield can be 100 percent effective.

The good news, however, is that it *is* possible to prepare your child to resist temptation. You may have recognized the opening paragraphs of this chapter as a modified retelling of the biblical story of Joseph and Potiphar's wife in Genesis 39, and the "desired response" as Joseph's words in verse 9. As he showed, godly young people can do the right thing in the face of sexual temptation.

How do we train children to hold a healthy, biblical view of sex and to want to please God in the midst of a porn-filled, sexually charged society? That's what this chapter is all about. Since some exposure to porn is inevitable, let's prepare our children's minds and hearts to respond in a God-honoring way.

WHERE TO BEGIN

Writing in his thoughtful book *False Intimacy*, Dr. Harry W. Schaumburg offers good counsel for how parents can prepare their kids mentally and spiritually for pure living in a morally polluted world. It starts, he says, with parents first developing their own vibrant relationship with Jesus Christ. When Mom and Dad love God, enjoy Him, believe that His instructions for living are in their best interests, and desire to please Him, their children will want to do the same.

Parents must not *assume* that this transference of faith is taking place, however. They need to make sure their kids are growing a genuine faith that will stand the tests of time and temptation. Kids who have a personal relationship with Jesus, understand their value as children of God, and know that they're loved are far less likely to be drawn in by pornographic materials. (For more about helping children develop such a faith, see Focus on the Family's *Parents' Guide to the Spiritual Growth of Children* and *Parents' Guide to the Spiritual Mentoring of Teens.*)

Next, parents need to model healthy sexual and interpersonal relationships in their own lives. As we saw in chapter 4, healthy relationships within the family are vital to the emotional, mental, and spiritual health of a child. So as a quick checkpoint, ask yourself, *Am I open and appropriately intimate in my relationships? Is the atmosphere in my home encouraging? Does my child feel appreciated and valued?*

If those qualities don't permeate a family—if instead there are fear of intimacy, feelings of abandonment, lack of appreciation, and loneliness—that home is fertile ground for sexually addictive behaviors. A child living there may begin searching for a sense of acceptance, safety, and intimacy in other ways, possibly including pornographic materials.

Assuming your family is basically healthy, however, the next part of the picture is communicating easily and well about sexual matters. Your child needs to know that she can talk about *anything* with you without being judged or put down—that she has total freedom to confide in you. She may be hearing things at school that upset her. Or she may have seen something on television that has confused her. You want to be the person she can confidently approach with her questions and concerns.

As parents, we should always be prepared to discuss sexual matters with our kids. They're bombarded with sexual images every day, so it's likely they'll be trying to process what they're seeing and hearing. We can help them make sense out of it all.

When you watch a TV program as a family, for example, take time afterward to discuss the male-female relationships in the show. Were these relationships God-honoring? Did the characters show respect for one another? Every show is a moral tale and, therefore, a chance to teach your child about morality.

Opportunities like that are known as "teachable moments." You can use them to spark a conversation with questions such as "How do you feel when you see that?" "Have others been talking to you about these things?" "How could the characters have made better decisions?" These questions can lead into discussions about sexual matters, temptation, pornography, lust, and so on.

To further help you prepare to take advantage of teachable moments, we've put together a series of suggested conversation starters that you can use as the opportunities present themselves. We've given you a lot of information in each of these. Our goal is not to overload you but to provide enough discussion points so you can carry on a worthwhile conversation with your child. You'll want to modify these in your own way,

---

Always Take a Kid Along

A dad named Jim Weidmann explains one of the ways in which he creates opportunities for the spiritual training/preparation of his kids:

"Hey, Jake. Put your shoes on. Let's get going."

"Okay, Dad."

It's Saturday: errand day for Dad. The van needs an oil change. A trip to the hardware store for screws and pipes and gadgets for the latest home improvement project: The perfect time for a one-on-one with one of the kids.

My dad taught me that. "Never go anywhere without a child," he told me. And he's right. By taking a kid away from the siblings, I get his or her full attention, and the child gets mine. I'm building the relationship while setting up the impromptu times. These are the moments when life presents the questions either from me or from the child, and the answers come from our faith view. The principle is that I must develop the relationship, for the relationship gives me the ability to share spiritual truth.[1]

rewording or deleting whatever you feel is not needed or appropriate to your child's age.

Age-Appropriateness

In deciding what's appropriate for your child, remember that kids are being exposed to pornography as young as four and five years of age. (And, of course, they're probably seeing sexually oriented material before that on TV, in ads, and elsewhere.) Because kids are now being sexualized so early, parents need to begin discussing sexuality (and pornography) as soon as they become aware that their children have been exposed to explicit materials, or as soon as their kids start asking questions about sexual matters.

Regrettably, Hollywood, the advertising industry, the porn business, and sex educators in our public schools now determine when you'll have to discuss sexual issues with your child. Your son or daughter *will* be exposed. You will need to respond as quickly as this becomes evident to you.

How explicit should you be? No matter what your child's age, there's no need to go into great detail about the various acts that take place in pornographic materials. A child *does* need to understand that sexual intercourse is only to take place between a husband and wife. In addition, this act is to be done in private; it's not something that should be filmed and shown to others.

If you haven't already had your basic "sex talk" with your child, you may want to do so as soon as possible. Once you've laid the groundwork that sexual intimacy is only for husbands and wives, and described the biological functions related to reproduction, you'll have an easier time dealing with "porn talk."

You might want to review briefly each of the conversation starter sections on the following pages. Then concentrate on the one that would be of the greatest immediate benefit to your child.

A Conversation Starter to Explain
God's Plan for Sex

This conversation may be sparked by something your child picks up at school from a teacher or fellow student. Or he may ask "sex" questions because of something he saw on TV or in a movie. You'll be far more at ease when these questions come if you've done some preparation. You can begin with a simple discussion of Adam and Eve and move into the reproductive process from that point.

◆ ◆ ◆

Main Discussion Point

God created Adam and Eve and blessed their marriage. He told them to reproduce and fill the earth. Satan, however, lured them into disobeying God, and, as a result, sin came into the world. For our own good, God wants only married people to have sex together, in private, but Satan wants unmarried people to have sex. He also wants people to look at pictures of naked people in magazines, movies, and on the Internet. To protect our hearts, minds, and spirits, God forbids us from looking at such things.

When God created the first man and woman, He named them Adam and Eve and placed them in a beautiful garden. Adam and Eve were both naked, but this was okay because they had no knowledge of evil yet and they were married.

Talking Point: It is God's plan that only men and women who are married to each other can sleep together without any clothes on. When God put Adam and Eve in the garden, He told them they could eat from any tree except the Tree of the Knowledge of Good and Evil. He wanted them to enjoy the garden and His company, but Satan had other ideas. He tricked Eve into disobeying God by getting her to eat the forbidden fruit. She then gave it to Adam, who willfully partook.

What is sin? According to God's Word, sin is rebellion or disobedience against God. Satan first rebelled against God because he wanted to rule over God's creation. He convinced other angels to join his rebellion, and they were all cast out of the presence of God in heaven.

Satan's goal, from the beginning of creation, was to cause men and women, boys and girls to rebel against God, too. Once Satan succeeded in getting Adam and Eve to sin, this rebellious tendency was passed along to the entire human race and became known as the "sin nature." We all have the inclination to sin against God and against our parents, neighbors, and friends.

Those who produce pornography are doing what their sin nature wants them to do. They are rebelling against God and tempting adults and kids to join their rebellion. When we look at photos or videos of men and women engaging in sexual intercourse, we are disobeying God.

Talking Point: God created an amazing way for human beings to have children. It's called the reproductive system, and it requires both a mother and a father to make a baby. The father has sperm inside his body in the scrotum, a sack that hangs below the penis. A sperm looks like a little tadpole with a tail that pushes it through a liquid called semen. The mother has special eggs inside her body. For a baby to be created, the sperm from the father has to reach an egg inside the mother's body.

This is done through sexual intercourse. The father places his penis inside the mother's vagina, and the sperm come out of the penis in the semen, travel up through the mother's vagina and uterus, and find the egg. A sperm then pushes its way inside the egg to fertilize it. When the egg is fertilized, a baby is created and begins to grow inside the mother's womb, a warm place where the child grows for nine months before being born. The baby comes out of the woman's vagina during birth.

God had a wonderful plan for sexual intercourse, and He blesses it when it is done by a husband and wife. He knows that any other use or depiction of sex harms us far more than it might give us pleasure.

Talking Point: Unfortunately, many people in the

world love doing bad things and disobeying God. Some of these people are called pornographers. They like to show men and women, boys and girls pictures of naked women and men. If someone shows you pictures of naked people, you're seeing something God knows you shouldn't.

Conversation Starter to Show Children That They Must Guard Their Hearts and Minds

♦ ♦ ♦

Main Discussion Point

God wants us to look at and think about only good things. He doesn't want us to look at bad pictures or be influenced by bad friends. When we see naked people in pictures or on TV, we may be tempted to do or to think about doing the same things they're doing. Our brain is like a huge, complex computer that records everything we see and hear. The images that go into our minds stay with us forever. This is why God wants us to flee from things that entice us to sin against Him and not allow ungodly images to enter our minds.

Let's discuss what Jesus says about how we should guard our hearts and minds from being influenced to think or do bad things. In Matthew 6:22-23, Jesus said, "The eye is the lamp of the body. If your eyes are good, your whole body will be full of light. But if your eyes are bad, your whole body will be full of darkness. If then the light within you is darkness, how great is that darkness!" When we look at good things and think about good things, we're obeying God and He's pleased with us. But if we look at bad pictures on TV, on the Internet, in a magazine, or in movies, we're disobeying God and making Him unhappy. He also wants us to read good books and have good friendships. If we keep reading or looking at bad things—or if we have bad friends—we will eventually be tempted to think and do something bad ourselves. When that happens, we have allowed darkness to come into our hearts.

Talking Point: Why does God want you to avoid looking at pictures of naked men, women, and children? He wants to protect you from seeing things that will always be inside your mind. These bad pictures can make you feel uncomfortable and even give you nightmares. And the longer you look at pictures like these, the more you will revisit them in your mind in the future and the more tempted you may be to do what you saw in the pictures.

Talking Point: In the Bible book of 2 Timothy, God tells us to avoid temptations. He says, "Flee the evil desires of youth, and pursue righteousness, faith, love and peace, along with those who call on the Lord out of a pure heart" (2:22).

Sexual temptations start in your mind when you watch things on TV you shouldn't be watching—or look at naked people on the Internet at a friend's house. The more you watch, the more you begin to think that what you're seeing is normal. And the longer you watch, the more likely you are to want to experiment with what you're seeing.

Talking Point: Your mind is a wonderful creation from God. The brain is like a huge computer that never needs to be plugged in and never has to be upgraded with a larger hard drive. The most amazing thing about the brain is that it retains every image that goes into it. Everything you see during a day is stored away in your brain. You can recall things that happened last week or last year, and those images will pop into your head immediately. This is both good and bad, depending on what you look at.

Think of a scary movie you may have seen recently—you can immediately remember the terrifying images you saw. Your brain has just recalled those images, and you can see them as clearly as when you watched them. You're also experiencing feelings. In fact, you may be feeling sick right now because your mind is replaying some frightening scene in a movie.

Talking Point: Can a movie create happy thoughts and feelings in your mind? How do you feel when you think about movies like *A Bug's Life, Muppets from Space,* or *Babe?* What kind of feelings do you have now? You see, the pictures you put into your head can influence how you think and how you feel. *You can also be influenced to act on your feelings.*

Here's an example of how a picture can influence you to do something: Have you ever watched a TV commercial for McDonald's Happy Meals? It makes you want to eat one of their hamburgers and some fries, doesn't it? That's the whole reason McDonald's puts ads on TV, and it works.

Now, what if you had a weight problem and you were trying to go on a diet? Imagine if you spent all your spare time sitting in McDonald's, watching every other kid eating Happy Meals, apple pies, and McFlurry ice cream treats. Would that help you with your diet, or would it just make it harder for you to say no to fattening foods? Of course it would make it harder.

The men and women who make pornographic movies are trying to do the same thing to you. They want to tempt you to watch things you shouldn't because they know you'll eventually become addicted to using their products. Then you'll be their customer for years to come. And just like the pushers of illegal drugs, pornographers don't care that using their products might ruin your life.

Talking Point: As we discussed in chapter 1, those who get involved in viewing pornography usually develop what is known as the Centerfold Syndrome. You can explain to your child that this creates a selfish attitude in boys and men, so that they only want to look at women rather than have caring relationships with them. Women become nothing more than objects for giving pleasure, rather than individuals with characters, souls, and spirits made in the image of God. This attitude dehumanizes women and frequently leads to their abuse.

EXPLAINING THE DANGERS
OF PORNOGRAPHY

Reread the section on the Centerfold Syndrome in chapter 1, and then describe to your child the dangers of being exposed to soft-core porn. Your child needs to understand that this subtle process first creates a false image of women. The images presented in pornography are lies. Real women come in all shapes and sizes, just as do real men. Women and men also age. No one ever stays perfectly physically fit, yet these images create the illusion that men have a right to a woman with a perfectly formed body.

Your child needs to understand that he must avoid believing lies or accepting fantasies into his mind about women and how they should look or act. A person's life is shaped by his attitudes, and his attitudes should be based on truth.

Second, explain to your child that pornographers are exploiting people for their own gain and encouraging their customers to do the same. Pornography is inherently selfish because its only purpose is to create a person who is obsessed with his own pleasure—and views others as objects to be used for pleasure.

Has your child ever known a neighborhood pal who used him for what he could get from him, not offering a true friendship? Has your son's "friend" wanted to come to your house just because your child had a PlayStation? This is using another person for selfish reasons, and God considers it a sin.

Third, help your child understand that porn is destructive to a wholesome and God-honoring future. A young man who continually views porn will expect sexual acts from his future wife that are unrealistic or that she might find unpleasant. He will probably also compare his wife to pornographic images he has seen, and she will invariably lose the competition. He will also have learned to fulfill his need for intimacy through magazines, videos, or the Internet, and he will avoid true intimacy with his spouse. His heart will become hardened, his conscience seared.

Conversation Starter on the Bible and Sexual Sin

◆ ◆ ◆

Main Discussion Point

God's Word warns us against sexual sins. These include looking at pictures of naked people, having sexual intercourse before you're married, committing adultery in marriage, and lust (imagining yourself naked and having sex with someone other than your spouse).

The Bible is clear that while sex is a wonderful gift meant to be enjoyed by husbands and wives, in any other context it is a sin. Consider just a few of the many relevant passages:

Exodus 20:14: "You shall not commit adultery."

Proverbs 6:24-25: "[Keep] … from the immoral woman, from the smooth tongue of the wayward wife.

Do not lust in your heart after her beauty or let her captivate you with her eyes."

Romans 6:13: "Do not offer the parts of your body to sin, as instruments of wickedness, but rather offer yourselves to God, as those who have been brought from death to life; and offer the parts of your body to him as instruments of righteousness."

1 Corinthians 6:13, 15, 18-20: "The body is not meant for sexual immorality, but for the Lord, and the Lord for the body.... Do you not know that your bodies are members of Christ himself? ... Flee from sexual immorality. All other sins a man commits are outside his body, but he who sins sexually sins against his own body. Do you not know that your body is a temple of the Holy Spirit, who is in you, whom you have received from God? You are not your own; you were bought at a price. Therefore honor God with your body."

Galatians 5:19: "Now the works of the flesh are evident, which are: adultery, fornication, uncleanness, lewdness" (NKJV).

God's Word is filled with stories of men and women who committed sexual sins and suffered for it. God's plan for families, on the other hand, is for a man and a woman to marry, have children (in most cases), and be faithful to each other as long as they live. They are not to commit adultery with other men or women. And single people are to remain sexually abstinent until they get married.

Talking Point: The Bible forbids adultery. What is adultery? It is sexual relations between a married person and someone other than his or her spouse. The Bible also forbids what is called *fornication*, which means sexual relations between people who are single.

People who produce pornography violate God's laws by showing unmarried people engaging in sex, as well as married men and women having sex with others who are not their spouses.

Talking Point: In addition, God forbids us from looking at porn because it strongly tempts us to commit adultery or fornication in our hearts with the people we see in those pictures. Jesus made it clear that in God's eyes, thinking favorably about doing something wrong is the same as actually doing it. He said in Matthew 5:27-28, "You have heard that it was said, 'Do not commit adultery.' But I tell you that anyone who looks at a woman lustfully has already committed adultery with her in his heart." Then He went on in verse 29 to give a serious warning about looking at things that cause you to commit adultery in your heart: "If your right eye causes you to sin, gouge it out and throw it away. It is better for you to lose one part of your body than for your whole body to be thrown into hell."

Jesus was saying that we must do everything we can to avoid looking at things that will cause us to have sexually sinful thoughts. By viewing pornography, we put bad pictures and bad thoughts into our minds—and they will never go away. We can't erase them or reformat them the way we can a computer disk or hard drive.

Conversation Starter on Fleeing from Temptation

♦ ♦ ♦

Main Discussion Point

God wants us to flee from temptation because He knows that giving in to sexual sin can damage our entire lives. Joseph is an example of a godly man who fled from temptation; King David is an example of someone who yielded to temptation and ruined his life and those of thousands of people around him.

ChristianAnswers.net, an Internet site providing biblical insights on moral issues, recently published an essay on sexual lust. In it, the author reprinted a poem, written anonymously, that paints a picture of what temptation is like once we start to give in. The poem goes like this:

> In the swamplands long ago,
> Where the weeds and mudglumps grow,
> A Yipiyuk bit on my toe ...
> Exactly why I do not know.
> I kicked and cried and hollered "Oh!"
> The Yipiyuk would not let go.
> I whispered to him soft and low.
> The Yipiyuk would not let go.
> Yes, that was sixteen years ago.
> And the Yipiyuk still won't let go.
> The snow may fall, the winds may blow.
> The Yipiyuk will not let go.

I drag him 'round each place I go,
And now, my child, at last you know
Exactly why I walk so slow.

The Yipiyuk can be a temptation you're always fighting against or a bad habit or lustful thought you may already have. If the writer of this poem had not been wandering through the swamp, he would not have been bitten by the Yipiyuk, and he wouldn't still have it hanging onto his toe. He should have stayed out of the swamp, which is a good picture of where pornography can lead you—into the muck, mire, and quicksand of ungodly thoughts and habits.

Is there a Yipiyuk in your life? How do you avoid getting one? The Bible gives us many examples of people who resisted temptation. It also tells stories of men and women who yielded to temptation and then carried a Yipiyuk around with them for the rest of their lives.

Remember the Danger

We take seriously the words of Dr. James Dobson at Focus on the Family's Pureintimacy.org Web site. He wrote: "Back in 1989, I interviewed convicted serial killer Ted Bundy on the eve of his execution in Florida. He shared with me how pornography pulled him out of a normal lifestyle and into a world of addiction and violence. Although many people are able to view pornography without following Bundy's murderous path, *few are able to escape the mental and emotional scars that change their view of sexuality and jeopardize their ability to have normal relationships*" (emphasis added).

Let's look first at the life of a young man who did the right thing.

Joseph: A Godly Man Who Fled from Sexual Sin

You may remember the story of Joseph, the boy who was sold into slavery by his own brothers and carried off to Egypt as a slave. Joseph was brought into the house of Potiphar, a powerful Egyptian official who worked for the pharaoh, or king, of Egypt. Potiphar was so impressed with Joseph's skills and integrity that he put him in charge of his whole household. Genesis 39 describes Joseph's life there. He had favor with God, and because of this, he was successful in everything he did.

Unfortunately, Potiphar's wife was not loyal to her husband and began trying to get Joseph to commit adultery with her. How did Joseph respond to this temptation? In verse 9 he told her, "My master has withheld nothing from me except you, because you are his wife. How then could I do such a wicked thing and sin against God?"

But Potiphar's wife didn't give up. Day after day, she tempted Joseph to go to bed with her. She was lusting after him and tried everything she could to seduce him into committing a sin against Potiphar and God.

Finally, one day she became so frustrated that she grabbed Joseph's coat when he was in the house and tried to drag him into bed. What did he do? He ran out of the house, leaving his coat behind.

He did the right thing by running away from sexual temptation, but Potiphar's wife was so angry at him that she falsely accused him of trying to seduce her. Potiphar threw him into prison.

Eventually, Joseph was freed from prison so he could help the pharaoh interpret a troubling dream. Because Joseph correctly interpreted the dream, the pharaoh told him, "Since God has made all this known to you, there is no one so discerning and wise as you. You shall be in charge of my palace, and all my people are to submit to your orders. Only with respect to the throne will I be greater than you" (Genesis 41:39-40).

In other words, the pharaoh put Joseph in charge of the entire nation of Egypt—one of the most powerful countries on the earth at that time. No one in the kingdom was more powerful except for the pharaoh. Joseph was rewarded by God because he had resisted temptation and remained faithful to Him.

Talking Point: Just like Joseph when he was thrown into prison for resisting temptation, you may suffer for doing the right thing if a friend tries to get you to look at pornographic pictures. You may be ridiculed and ignored in school because you refuse to disobey God. If this happens, pray for the strength to keep on resisting temptation. But there may come a time when you have to do what Joseph did: *Run away from the temptation to sin.* You may also have to stop hanging around with bad friends. The Bible says in 1 Corinthians 15:33, "Do not be misled: 'Bad company corrupts good character.'" Proverbs 4:14 says, "Do not set foot on the path of the wicked or walk in the way of evil men." If you continue to spend time with kids who tempt you to do bad things, you may eventually give in and join them.

Talking Point: If you're tempted to look at pornography, do what Joseph did: First, he resisted. Then, when it became clear that he was being literally dragged into sexual sin, he ran away.

If you have friends who are trying to get you to look at pornographic pictures on the Internet, in a magazine, or in a video, you can do these five things:

• Resist
• Look away
• Flee
• Tell your parents what happened
• Pray with your mom and dad that you will have the strength to resist temptation in the future

David: A Godly Man Who Fell into Sexual Sin
The Bible calls King David the "apple of God's eye" (see Psalm 17:8). As a boy, he was handpicked by God to become the king of Israel. David wrote many of the beautiful psalms we read in the Bible; a number of them have been made into songs we sing in church each week.

David truly loved God. Unfortunately, a time came in David's life when he committed a terrible sin against God, against a loyal soldier named Uriah, and against Uriah's wife, Bathsheba. We find the story in 2 Samuel 11.

It was in the springtime, when most kings who lived during those times led their soldiers off to battle. This year, however, David stayed home and sent his generals to lead the army of Israel against its enemies. He was idle, and he soon got into trouble.

Verses 2-3 tell us what happened: "One evening David got up from his bed and walked around on the roof of the palace. From the roof he saw a woman bathing. The woman was very beautiful, and David sent someone to find out about her."

The woman was Bathsheba, and David, filled with lust, had her brought into his palace and then had sex with her. He was already married, and he knew she was too, but he committed adultery with her anyway. This sin would have terrible consequences for David and his family.

He soon learned that she had become pregnant with his child, and he decided to try to keep his sin secret. He had Uriah brought back from the battlefield, thinking Uriah would sleep with Bathsheba and then believe that the baby was his own.

The plan didn't work. Uriah, unlike David, had a great sense of duty, and he told David he couldn't enjoy his wife's company while the rest of the army was still fighting. David convinced him to stay in Jerusalem one more day. He then got Uriah drunk, hoping that in that condition he would go home to sleep with his wife. Even drunk, however, Uriah didn't go home. Instead, he slept on a mat with the palace servants. Finally, in a last attempt to hide his first sin, David sent Uriah back into battle in such a way that guaranteed Uriah would be killed.

Talking Point: David's adultery was bad enough,

but then he multiplied his sins by having Bathsheba's husband killed. What began as a lustful thought in his mind ended up in murder! Sin is like that. It can begin as a seemingly insignificant thing but then grow into something terrible. If you feed sin, it will grow.

Talking Point: What happened to David and Bathsheba after this? Uriah was killed as David had planned, and David then married Bathsheba. Their baby boy was born, but he soon died. Later, one of David's sons would rape one of his stepsisters. Another son named Absalom would seize control of Jerusalem while trying to remove King David from his throne. David would have to flee from the city to avoid being killed. A terrible war would then be fought between David's men and Absalom's, and more than 20,000 would die in battle. Eventually, four of David's sons were to die.

All this happened because David lusted after a woman, took her to bed with him, got her pregnant, and killed her husband to cover up his sin.

Talking Point: What did David do wrong in the very beginning of this sad story? He was *idle*; he *looked* at a naked woman; he *lusted* after her; and then he *acted* on his lust and slept with her.

What *should* he have done? Well, in the first place, he probably should have led his army into battle instead of remaining in Jerusalem. But then, when he saw Bathsheba bathing, he should have *looked away* immediately and *run* back into his palace. He should have *fled* from sexual temptation, but instead he ran toward it.

Talking Point: This story shows us that you must

be careful where you go and what you look at. Don't go to places physically, like the home of a friend who you know has pornographic pictures, or to places on TV or the Internet where you'll be exposed to things you shouldn't see. If you watch where you go, you can avoid a lot of temptations, tears, and trouble.

Second, if you do see something you know you shouldn't, look away and then flee from the situation as soon as you can. Afterward, tell your parents about your experience so they can pray with you that God will help you continue to avoid temptation in the future.

THE "PORN TALK"

Dr. Mark Laaser, in *Talking to Your Kids About Sex,* observed, "Without question, exposing children to pornography will make them more likely to look at it again, but talking to them about it, even sharing one's own story about it, takes the mystery away. Satan works on the naturally curious mind, tempting it to find out what it knows nothing about." In discussing the subject with your kids, Laaser suggests that both Mom and Dad be involved, so that both a male and a female perspective are offered. Mom can express her feelings about how pornography treats women as less than human, as nothing more than sex objects meant for pleasing men, rather than as creations of God with feelings and a need to be valued as whole people. Dad can discuss the lasting effects porn has on boys and men.

Specifically, Laaser suggests emphasizing the following talking points:

◆ Your goal as a young person is to develop a strong personal relationship with Jesus Christ. That includes obeying what God's Word says about sexual purity and holiness because He wants only the best for you.

◆ One of your goals may also be to get married, have kids, and live faithfully with your spouse for the rest of your life. But if you start viewing pornography, it can affect how you view your own wife or husband and destroy your chances of developing an intimate, loving relationship with your spouse.

◆ Another goal should be to live a life of personal integrity and honesty before all people. Pornography will lead you to live a life of deceit and moral corruption.

◆ Porn can lead you into sexual sin, addiction, sexually transmitted diseases, and even molestation or other sex crimes. Pornography can also distort your conscience and sense of right and wrong. It can harm all of your relationships.[2]

WHAT TO TELL YOUR CHILDREN ABOUT MOLESTATION AND SEXUAL PREDATORS

Pornography is used by pedophiles to desensitize children to nudity and sexual activities between adults and children. As you prepare to discuss this with your child, consider the following comment from San Diego FBI agent John Ianarelli: "The Internet has become the playground of the 21st century. Instead of hanging out in the park, the guy in the overcoat you used to worry about is hanging out on the Internet, where he figures he doesn't have to worry about who's watching him."

Ianarelli regularly goes on the Internet and poses as a 10-year-old boy or a 12-year-old girl. In an interview in the *San Diego Union-Tribune* on July 9, 2000, Ianarelli said, "I can go into a chat room and ask the most innocent kind of question about sports or something else. Within minutes, you'll have people coming out of the woodwork at you with sexual innuendoes, sexual invitations."

San Diego law enforcement officers are being trained to track "cyberstalkers"—individuals who prey on young children and teens. In just this one city, their sex crimes unit is seeing a dramatic increase in the number of "travelers" on the Web. These are men who establish contact with children over the Internet and then either travel to meet them or pay for the child to run away from home to meet them somewhere for sexual contact.

What Is a Pederast or Pedophile?

There are basically two kinds of child molesters. One is called a *pederast*. This is a homosexual man or woman who has fixated on children or teens as the object of sexual desire. The other is called a *pedophile* and prefers opposite-sex children, though the term *pedophile* is typically used to describe both homosexual and heterosexual molesters.

Researcher Dr. Gene Abel once interviewed hundreds of pedophiles to compare molestation rates between homosexuals and heterosexuals. He talked with 153 self-confessed pederasts, who admitted to molesting a total of 22,981 victims. That's 150 boys per molester. He also interviewed 224 heterosexual pedophiles, who admitted to molesting 4,435 girls. That's 19.8 girl victims per molester. The difference is dramatic.

More than 90 percent of all molestations are committed by men. However, as lesbianism is popularized in our public schools, we may see the rate of lesbian-induced sexual molestations rise. The homosexual teachers' organization Gay, Lesbian and Straight Education Network (GLSEN) is promoting the establishment of Gay-Straight Alliance clubs on school campuses. Older homosexuals who serve as "mentors" in these clubs will have the opportunity to seduce sexually confused children and pull them into a lifestyle that can result in severe mental problems and even death from AIDS. More than 700 of these clubs already exist on campuses through the U.S., and the numbers are growing. These clubs serve as perfect cover for men and women who seek to have sexual contact with children.

Homosexuals have long sought to have the "age of consent" lowered so they can have intercourse with children. Dozens of Web sites track age-of-consent laws in the U.S. and overseas. They also list vacation spots where gay men can freely access boys for sexual encounters.

A Conversation Starter on Child Molesters

Begin by telling your children that God has given you, the parent, the job of protecting them. And just as you make sure they're safe when crossing the street or getting too close to a hot stove, so you also need to protect them by warning them that there are evil people in the world who would like to hurt them. They may meet these people in the park, in school, on the playground, in church, in sports, or on the Internet.

They will be able to spot these bad people not by how they look but by what they try to show them. *The pedophile uses a standard routine in seducing a child.* He begins by befriending the child in some way, often including gifts. He may start showing the child pictures of kids in underwear from Sears catalogs or other seemingly harmless publications. The goal is to desensitize the child over a period of months until he is ready to engage in sexual contact. The progression goes from underwear pictures to pictures of naked men, women, and children in family poses. Next, he progresses to showing the child pictures of adults and children touching each other. The child is told, "See, this is what Mommy and Daddy do. Isn't this fun?" After that, the molester will show the child pictures of adults and children engaging in sexual acts. "Doesn't that look like fun?" he'll ask. "Why don't you and I play a game like that?"

The pedophile will, of course, caution the child to keep this a secret. A more brazen molester might even threaten to hurt or kill the child if he tells his parents.

The seduction process can also take place on the Internet. The pedophile can send photos to the child so he can download the material onto his computer. In many cases, the pedophile will eventually try to make arrangements to meet the child for a sexual encounter.

What if your child meets a sexual predator on the Internet? What if a neighbor tries to get him to look at naked men, women, and children? What if a trusted adult, such as a church youth leader, makes sexual advances?

Remind your children that you're there to keep them safe from people who would try to hurt them. They also need to know you're not going to be mad at them if they find themselves targeted by a sexual predator.

A Conversation Starter on Safety Tips

Here are some simple instructions to give your child for dealing with molesters or cyberstalkers:

1. If anyone you know or anyone you encounter on the Internet begins talking to you about sexual matters, tell us immediately! If anyone touches you in places where you know he shouldn't, tell us!

2. If someone asks you to keep a secret about his sexual comments—or if someone on the Internet sends you pictures of naked people—tell us immediately.

3. Don't ever agree to meet someone in person that you've met online.

4. Don't give out your home address, phone number, computer password, name of your school, or any other kind of personal information to people on the Internet.

5. Don't ever respond to or even open E-mail messages that have sexual comments in the subject line. Come and tell us immediately (and then you should report it to the police).

6. Don't ever send pictures of yourself to strangers.

7. If a friend tries to show you pornography on the Internet, tell us immediately and we'll talk to his parents about it.

Especially for Girls

So far in this book we've talked mostly about the visual images that people usually think of as pornography, images found in magazines, videos, Web sites, and so on. But if your child is a girl, and you're preparing her to stay pure in our X-rated culture, you need to be aware that males and females are wired differently. Consequently, the dangers they face are different.

Boys and men are stimulated sexually by visual images, and thus they're the primary users of porn. Women, on the other hand, are primarily stimulated emotionally. Thus, women and girls are more likely to frequent Internet chat rooms looking for relationships. And while at first glance that may seem to be a harmless activity, it actually entails considerable danger.

As Alvin Cooper, clinical director of the San Jose (Calif.) Marital and Sexuality Centre, put it, "The Internet provides a way that women can experiment and be free to explore, but it's also getting a lot of them into trouble."[3] And as Focus on the Family points out in its online publication "Resources for Online Sexual Addiction," "Online relationships often evolve rapidly and passionately as women search for the communication and intimacy that may be missing from their life in the real world. Young girls often go into chat rooms and end up flirting with more boldness and openness than they would ever show off-line."[4]

The news media have recounted numerous cases where lonely girls have actually run away from home to meet boys they've met in a chat room. Frequently, these girls have discovered that their idealized lover on the Web was actually a pedophile. In fact, police officers who deal with online sex crimes view chat rooms as the new school playground for pedophiles and other sexual predators.

Accordingly, you will want to warn your daughter about revealing too much personal information or getting too involved with someone she meets online. You should also set strict guidelines about what kind of chat rooms your children can access and how much time they can spend there. It would be wise for you to access a teen chat room yourself just to see what's being discussed.

The Internet isn't the only danger for a girl seeking emotional connection, either. As noted by Sara June Davis and Lindy Beam, writing in the Focus publication *Fantasy World: Pure Thinking in a Sea of Unrealistic Images*, women "love romance and long for intimacy. Because of this built-in drive, we are most easily affected by the pollutants that play to our imagination and ideals. Romance novels, television, movies, online relationships and teen magazines—'harmless' stuff that we see every day—can distort our view of sex, love, marriage, and men by flooding us with false images. It might even be called pornography for the mind and emotions."[5]

Thus, you'll want to talk with your daughter about the messages concerning love and sex that are found in romance novels, MTV, teen magazines, TV programs, and movies. These can all provide girls with unrealistic thoughts about sexuality. But by taking advantage of teachable moments, you can help your child to separate the lies from the truth.

BUILDING SPIRITUAL STRENGTH

A key part of preparing your child's mind and heart to deal properly with pornography is to help him develop spiritual strength ahead of time. Just as a virus has a harder time getting a grip on a healthy body than it does on one that's already weakened, so also a child who has made habits of reading God's Word, talking with Him about everything in prayer, and seeking to please Him will be better able to withstand the lure of porn.

As the parent, you play the most important role in helping your child develop this kind of spiritual power. Your own example of praying, reading Scripture, and living to please God will set the pattern. That, plus your loving encouragement for your child to do the same, along with your instruction in teachable moments, will help your child to make those habits a part of her own life. In addition, you can promote times of family prayer, Scripture memorization, and Christian fellowship. (For more about helping your child to grow spiritually, we again recommend Focus on the Family's Heritage Builders resources, especially the *Parents' Guide to the Spiritual Growth of Children* and the *Parents' Guide to the Spiritual Mentoring of Teens.*)

Teach your child the strategy for dealing with temptation that we saw earlier in the conversation starter on the subject: *Resist. Look away. Flee. Tell your parents what happened. Pray with your mom and dad that you will have the strength to resist temptation in the future.* If your child has internalized this response before temptation actually arises, he won't have to try to figure out what to do when the time comes; he'll be able to respond quickly and appropriately.

USING MOVIES TO REINFORCE THE MESSAGE

Since children typically love to watch movies, we suggest you put them to good use as part of preparing your child for life in today's world. A number of films deal with sexual temptation and show what can happen when a person yields to that enticement. We briefly describe some of these below for your consideration. You'll want to preview each of them before you decide whether to show them to your child, as some may be too complex for younger kids to understand. You'll have to make that determination based on the maturity level of each child. We have not included any movies containing explicit sexual content.

♦ *Mr. Holland's Opus.* Mr. Holland, a music teacher, is briefly tempted by one of his students to run away with her to New York to pursue a career on Broadway.

♦ *Anna and the King.* Anna is a teacher who moves to Thailand in the 1800s with her son, and she tutors the king's children. Both she and the king are tempted to become romantically involved, but her Christian beliefs help her to resist. The film also shows how one person's good works can influence others around her to do good, too.

♦ *Left Behind.* This film, based on Tim LaHaye and Jerry Jenkins's best-selling novel about the end times, tells the story of an airline pilot who has been having an affair with a stewardess. After the Rapture of the church—including his own wife—the pilot repents and accepts Jesus Christ as Savior. This is a great story of repentance and restoration!

♦ *Bad Company.* This is an older film, set in the Wild West. A young Christian boy teams up with a robber played by Jeff Bridges. The boy eventually succumbs to his partner's evil influence, which illustrates a strong biblical message: Bad company corrupts good morals.

♦ *Joseph.* This made-for-TV movie is one of the most

accurate portrayals of Joseph's life ever done. It shows him being tempted by Potiphar's wife and resisting her advances. There is a scene of Joseph's wife bathing that may not be appropriate for younger children.

♦ *The Natural.* Robert Redford stars in this film about a talented baseball player who yields to sexual temptation. His career is destroyed for years because of his failure to resist, but it is eventually redeemed.

♦ *Moby Dick.* This classic Herman Melville story, starring Gregory Peck, shows the dangers of seeking revenge and how one man's sin can affect everyone around him. (Captain Ahab's sins lead to the deaths of all but one of his ship's crew.)

QUESTIONS TO ASK ABOUT THIS CHAPTER

Once you finish going through the conversation starters, you may want to consider asking your child some or all of the following questions. They will provoke more thought and reinforce the lessons you've taught. As we've suggested before, take advantage of teachable moments that present themselves so you can discuss things in a relaxed, unforced way—perhaps after watching one of the films in the preceding section.

1. What is God's perfect plan for sex? [Possible answer: God's perfect plan is that men and women will marry, have sexual relations, and remain faithful as long as they live.]

2. What is Satan's desire for you? [Possible answer: To get you to disobey God by getting involved in pre-marital relationships or becoming hooked on porn. His ultimate desire is to keep you separated from God so you will end up in hell.]

3. David yielded to the temptation to commit adultery with another man's wife, and his sin resulted in terrible things for her, their baby, and his nation. What was the first mistake he made? [Possible answer: He was in the wrong place and yielded to temptation when he saw Bathsheba bathing.]

4. David thought about sinning, then acted on it. What have you done that you've thought about and then taken action on—even though you knew it was wrong? Did you get away with it? Did God see you?

5. After David got Bathsheba pregnant, what should he have done? [Possible answer: He should have repented and not plotted to have her husband killed.]

6. What does this story tell you about the consequences of sin? Did God forgive David? [Possible answer: You can still be forgiven by God, but the consequences of sin can last for years.]

7. Are we always rewarded for doing the right thing? Discuss what happened to Joseph. [Possible answer: Even though we may suffer for doing the right thing, God still wants us to obey Him. Jesus was crucified for doing good. We must trust that God will make something good come out of even the worst situation.]

8. How did God reward Joseph for his obedience?

[Possible answer: He made him second only to the pharaoh in Egypt.]

9. What should motivate us to avoid temptation? [Possible answers: Our love of God, our concern for hurting others, knowing what's best for ourselves, fear of punishment.]

10. What steps do we need to take to resist temptation? [Possible answer: Avoid it, run from it, and tell others about our struggles.]

11. What should you do if you yield to temptation and look at something you shouldn't? Should you hide what you did, like David? [Possible answer: You should tell your parents what you saw, ask for forgiveness, and make every effort to avoid the temptation in the future.]

12. Have you ever given in to temptation? Have you resisted temptation? Why?

13. Pictures affect our thoughts. What do you see in your mind when I say "Muppets"? What kind feelings do you have when I say "Jurassic Park"? Do you see how images can influence your emotions?

14. Why should we avoid looking at pornography? [Possible answer: Because God wants us to remain pure and holy in His sight. He doesn't want us to become addicted to porn or to develop the wrong ideas about God's plan for sex between a husband and wife.]

15. Is there a Yipiyuk in your life? What is it?

16. What should you do if someone makes sexual comments to you on the Internet? [Possible answer: Tell your parents and report the incident to the police.]

CHAPTER SIX

Practical Steps to Keep Pornography Out of Your Home

Several years ago, my wife and I (Frank) subscribed to DirectTV in order to get better reception and a wider choice of programming. As part of the sign-up package, we were automatically given a 30-day preview of several movie networks. I was channel surfing through the movies one evening and landed on Cinemax. With a jolt, I quickly realized I was seeing a pornographic movie, as a man began pouring chocolate sauce over a naked woman. I called DirectTV immediately and had them disconnect the premium movie channels from my service.

Preparing our children's hearts and minds for life in

an X-rated world is an essential first step, as we saw in chapter 5. However, we can do much more to protect them. Human nature being what it is, we're all vulnerable to sexual temptations, no matter how strongly we believe in holiness and purity. If we as adults can fall, how much more vulnerable are our children? And as my experience with Cinemax shows, porn can find its way into our homes without our even being aware of it if we're not careful.

Thus, the purpose of this chapter is to help you be more aware of ways in which pornography might find its way into your own home and how you can safeguard your family. In the following sections, we'll describe some practical strategies and tools you can use to put a hedge of protection between your child and the sexual predators who push porn.

WHAT OR WHO IS REACHING YOUR CHILD?

To protect your child from pornography, you need to know what influences are reaching him, both in your home and when he ventures outside. Here are a few things to consider:

◆ Do you know your child's friends and their parents? Do they share your values? What kind of influences are available in their homes? For instance, do your child's friends have unlimited access to pornography on the Internet or through pay-per-view TV movies? Do the parents allow their children to watch

R- or NC-17-rated movies? (You'd be surprised how many parents do.)

• Do you know where your child goes after school or in the evenings? Does he hang out at comic book stores? Might she be going to movies without your consent? Does he play violent video games at the local mall arcade?

• Do you have ground rules established for what your child is allowed to watch outside the home? For example, you may want to establish a rule that your child must call home to ask for permission before he views a movie. If you're unfamiliar with the movie, err on the side of safety and ask that your child come home. You may also access Ted Baehr's MovieGuide Web site

Her Addiction Began at Home

Martha's involvement with pornography began in her own home when she discovered that her parents had a hidden stash of magazines. Later, her descent accelerated through the seemingly innocuous avenue of reading romance novels in high school. According to Martha, "I was addicted to those. I would read every kind of romance novel, every trashy thing I could get my hands on. Then, when I went into college, I started subscribing to *Playgirl*. At 19, I started dating an elementary school teacher I had met at a bar. He was in his late 30s, and he showed me my first pornographic movie."

While Martha was in college, she lived at home. As soon as her new *Playgirl* would arrive in the mail, her mother would look through it. Thus, with the approval of her own mother, Martha became convinced that it was all right to consume pornographic materials.

(MovieGuide.org) or Focus on the Family's pluggedin-mag.com site to get a quick review of whatever movie your child wants to watch.

WHAT ABOUT TV AND VIDEOS?

Television presents some special challenges but also some encouraging opportunities to take a principled stand against the spread of pornography. Unfortunately, most cable companies and the two major satellite companies (Dish TV and DirectTV) carry pornographic programming. They typically offer the Playboy Channel and/or other, even more sexually explicit services such as Spice, Ecstasy, and The Hot Network. If you need cable or satellite TV to have decent reception or want a wide range of viewing options, you're probably going to have to subscribe to a service that also provides pornography to its customers. This may be a matter of serious moral compromise to you, and you may just opt to have a TV antenna.

If you do subscribe to a cable or satellite service, your provider will usually offer a parental control option. With it, you can block out unwanted channels by punching in the station number. Those channels will then be off-limits for everyone in the family.

Some networks you might want to consider blocking include E!, MTV, MTV2, and VH1, to name a few. Each of these companies offers a flood of improper sexual imagery. E!, for example, features Howard Stern and a regular feature called *Wild On...* that shows people engaging in sexually promiscuous conduct at vacation spots around the world. The music channels feature sexually oriented videos that leave little to the imagination. In addition, many of these videos combine violence with sex—a lethal combination that can seriously impair a viewer's sense of morality. If you've ever seen a Marilyn Manson video on MTV, you saw a disturbing combination of sex, violence, and Satan worship.

If you choose to block one or all of these stations, or others that you find dangerous to your child's moral health, request the blocking by contacting your cable/satellite provider. If you know which companies advertise on those channels, contacting them as well and tell them your concerns with the programming they sponsor, and that you're boycotting their company by blocking them out. The provider will lose revenue if many customers block channels, as they charge for advertising based on their estimated audience reach. And the advertisers may go elsewhere if they believe the cable company is driving away audiences with antisocial programming.

CHECKING FOR SIGNAL BLEED

Cable companies providing pornographic channels typically allow what is called "signal bleed" on their systems. This means that the company will scramble the signal of a pornography service or premium movie channel but not completely block out the image or sound. This is tempting for children, who can still hear the sounds of sexual activities and occasionally see a fairly clear picture—especially if there's a white background.

The Playboy Channel recently won a Supreme Court victory on signal bleed. Under a major provision of the 1996 Communications Decency Act, cable companies were required to carry sexually explicit programming only between 10 P.M. and 6 A.M. unless they could completely block both the sound and images from pornographic channels. The Court, however, ruled that this provision is unconstitutional. (See Appendix A for more information.)

As bad as that decision was for children, parents can still protect their kids if they will take advantage of the opportunity. Under section 504 of the 1996 Telecommunications Act, cable companies are required to provide total blocking for customers who want it. The law says, "Upon request by a cable service subscriber, a cable operator shall, without charge, fully scramble or otherwise fully block the audio and video programming of each channel carrying such programming so that ... a subscriber does not receive it." If enough concerned parents took advantage of this law, it could have the effect of driving pornographers from cable systems everywhere.

You may currently subscribe to a cable service that *appears* to block out pornography channels; if you scroll through the porn channel numbers, you get a blank screen. However, to be positive your cable system is fully blocking porn signals, punch in the channel number on your remote control. If a scrambled porn channel appears, you've got a problem. Try using the parental control device provided by your cable company to lock out access to the channel. If that fails, contact the company and insist that it install a full blocking device on your service.

MOVIE CHANNELS AND VIDEOS

If you subscribe to premium movie channels—especially HBO, ShowTime, or Cinemax—you're bringing R- and even hard-R-rated movies into your home. (A hard-R movie is actually an NC-17 [formerly X-rated] movie that has been slightly edited to avoid obscenity prosecution.) Cinemax is probably the worst offender with regard to the explicitness of the materials it shows; remember the story told at the start of this chapter.

If you have movie channels, you may want to block them out until you see a show in the newspaper listings that the entire family can watch together.

As for videos (and nowadays, DVDs), we assume you control what gets brought into your home for viewing on your living room VCR. But does your child have his own VCR in his bedroom? What kind of videos does he watch there? Is he borrowing videos from friends? Is he checking R-rated videos out of the library and viewing them? (According to American Library Association guidelines, you're not allowed to know what videos your child is checking out at your local library.) Don't assume that all is well. Remember that a VCR in a child's bedroom can easily become an open window into the world of pornography, and that porn is powerfully tempting.

SAFETY DEVICES FOR TV VIEWING

A whole array of electronic devices is being marketed today that can give you some peace of mind about the TV shows and movies that come into your home. As noted earlier, most cable and satellite companies have blocking options on their remote controls. A number of other systems can block out pornography channels, set time limits on TV watching, and even remove profanity from TV shows and movies. The list below is not an endorsement of particular products but simply a survey of available options.

The V-Chip. This device, attached to your TV, will read the ratings imbedded in TV shows of every kind. You can limit what your child can watch by keying in the highest rating you'll allow. If your child tries to access a show that exceeds that rating, a blank screen will appear.

TV Allowance. This product allows you to limit how much time each of your children can spend watching TV or playing video games. Each child is given a weekly "allowance" of time. When he or she comes to the end of that allowance, the TV goes blank and won't turn back on for that child until the beginning of the following week, when a new allowance is automatically made available.

TV Guardian and **CurseFree TV.** Both of these detect and filter profanity and blasphemy from TV programs, TV movies, and videos. Each product will substitute nonoffensive phrases in place of curse words or remarks that take the Lord's name in vain.

Home Movie Editor. This product equips you to remove offensive content from videos you purchase. Or, if you record movies from TV, you can edit those tapes to delete offensive scenes. A second way of editing your own videos is to purchase a VCR with two tape slots; one records and the other is used to duplicate and/or edit the video. A less-efficient way is to simply use your standard VCR and record over areas of a movie that may harm your child.

GOING TO THE MOVIES!

If you've watched many videos or attended many movies, you're already aware that the Motion Picture Association of America's (MPAA) rating system is worthless if you're concerned about sexual content. A PG-13-rated movie can contain nudity, while an R-rated movie may contain no nudity. The fact is that the rating system has probably done more harm than good. It serves as a temptation for children rather than as an accurate guide for parents.

What can you do? One of the best ways to keep your children from seeing movies that contain sexual and/or extremely violent content is to regularly read reviews offered by Christian organizations. A secular movie reviewer will probably not share your values concerning graphic sexual content or immoral messages, focusing instead on plot line, character development, and overall film quality. Fortunately, a number of reliable Christian film review sources exist. Here are several:

◆ The online version of Focus on the Family's *Plugged In* magazine (www.pluggedinmag.com) contains reviews of both older and current movies.

◆ Crosswalk.com features movie reviews, video releases, and a review archive.

◆ ChristianAnswers.net has an extensive movie review section.

◆ MovieGuide.org, founded by Ted Baehr, reviews movies before they're released.

◆ *World* magazine includes excellent movie reviews and other analyses of pop culture. Its Web site also has a searchable database you can use to locate reviews of movies that are no longer in theaters.

THE KID NEXT DOOR

You can do everything possible to keep porn out of your home, but you've still got to deal with the influence of the kid next door or around the corner who may be heavily into it. One mom cleansed her home of pornographic materials and subscribed to a Christian Internet provider (more about that option later in this chapter). However, her son was spending a great deal of time at a neighbor friend's home, where the two boys were allowed unfiltered and unsupervised Internet access. This mom spoke with the neighbor boy's mother and requested that her son not be allowed on the Internet at the neighbor's home. The other mother refused. Consequently, the first mom no longer lets her son go to that friend's home.

You may be facing a similar situation. If your child spends large amounts of time at a friend's house, you may wish to have a discussion about pornography with the parents. If those parents refuse to cooperate with your guidelines concerning TV, movies, magazines, the Internet, and so on, you may have to forbid your child from spending time in that home. This may cause hurt feelings and tension between the families, but your child's moral and emotional health are at stake.

TAKING SERIOUSLY THE INTERNET THREAT

As noted in an earlier chapter, a child can get into a pornography Web site within two clicks of a mouse. That fact should cause every parent to take the Internet threat very seriously indeed, because the things a child might find there are truly shocking.

To help you better understand the danger, let us

reiterate the nature of what's available to children online. Dr. James Dobson wrote about this issue after serving on a presidential commission on pornography. In *Pornography: A Human Tragedy*, he addressed all forms of porn, but everything he mentioned is on the Internet as well as elsewhere: "How can I describe that world [of hard-core pornography] without being obscene myself? ... I struggle at this moment as I weigh the terribleness of this subject against the need for Christians to understand their enemy.... X-rated movies and magazines today feature oral, anal, and genital sex between women and donkeys, pigs, horses, dogs, and dozens of other animals. . . ." Then he noted that other displays of pornography include urination, defecation, mutilation, and incest.

Dr. Dobson continued, "I want to give special emphasis to the harm associated with pornography that falls into the hands of children and adolescents. It would be extremely naïve for us to assume that the river of obscenity that has inundated the American landscape has not invaded the world of children. . . . What a tragedy! If the explicit descriptions I've offered in this chapter have been disturbing to you, the mature reader, imagine how much more destructive the actual visualizations are to children and adolescents. Teenagers especially are prone to imitate what they see and hear."[1]

To see for yourself just a little of what's out there, use your Internet search engine to do a simple search using word combinations like *teen* and *sex* or *nude,* and your screen will be filled with list after list of sites showing children in sexually explicit poses. A word search of *homosexual* and *teen* will bring up horrendous sites featuring every kind of sexual perversion. In addition, sites showcasing bestiality, bodily functions and sex, necrophilia, and every other kind of sexual deviation imaginable are readily accessible—plus some depravities you haven't imagined.

A few minutes of scanning through such lists should provide all the motivation you need to take actions that will protect your child.

SOME SIMPLE SOLUTIONS

Focus on the Family has published an online guide for parents to use in setting standards for Internet use. Here are some of those suggestions:

1. Keep the computer in a public area, like the family room or kitchen.

2. Show your children what to do if they accidentally stumble onto a bad site.

3. Set up ground rules for use of the computer, and stick to them. Let your children know the consequences that will follow misuse, then follow through if necessary.

4. Consider using filtering software that keeps a log of all the sites your family visits.

5. Don't use the computer as a baby-sitter. Set time limits on Internet usage, and discourage late-night use.

6. Don't talk to strangers; it's a rule that's as valid on the Internet as it is on the streets. The Internet hides the true identity of users, so there's no way to know if people are who they say they are.

7. Guard your family's privacy by never giving out your name, address, or telephone number (except, of course, when doing something like placing an order with an established retailer).

8. Don't allow children to reveal too much about themselves in the "personal profile" sections that some Internet companies provide. Pedophiles prey on this information. (Parents should become familiar with new rules for Web site operators, established by the Federal Trade Commission [FTC]. The Children's Online Privacy Protection Act [COPPA], effective April 2000, restricts how Web site operators may collect and use personal information from children under age 13. The rules spell out when and how these operators must seek parental consent and what responsibilities they have to protect your child's privacy and safety online. For more information, see the FTC's article "How to Protect Kids' Privacy Online" at www.ftc.gov ["Kidz Privacy" section, click on "Resources."]

9. Supervise your child's chat room activity. Pedophiles are lurking in chat rooms, especially where children gather.

10. Check the Internet history files regularly, and

perhaps even read E-mail if you have reason to suspect a problem.

11. Help children to set up "bookmarks" to enable easy access to positive, fun, and educational sites. Here are a few such sites that Focus on the Family provides: "Adventures in Odyssey"(www.whitsend.org), "Clubhouse"(www.clubhousemagazine.com), "Brio"(www.briomag.com), "Breakaway"(www.family.org/breakaway), and "Life on the Edge—Live!"(www.family.org/lote/lotelive).[2]

That second suggestion is a key point. Make sure your kids know how to get out of a bad site. Show them the Back button on the browser, which will take them back to the previous screen. They can also hit the Home key to return to the default home page on your computer. This is usually the home page of your Internet service provider (ISP). Unfortunately, as we saw in chapter 2, pornographers frequently take control of a computer's browser when someone stumbles onto their site. When the person tries to get out, another porn window appears on the screen—and still another. If your child finds himself caught in this predicament, tell him to shut the computer off and come tell you what happened. You can then reboot and find out what porn Web site had seized control of your browser.

Of course, to eliminate 99 percent of these problems, you should strongly consider purchasing a software filtering system or subscribing to an ISP that offers filtering from its mainframe computer.

WHAT IS FILTERING, AND HOW DOES IT WORK?

David Burt, a former librarian who now works for a major filtering system software company, described on his Web site how such systems work. He noted:

> Filtering software is designed to screen offensive content from users. This is accomplished using four basic methods: Blocking by address to create a "blacklist" or "stoplist"; blocking by word; blocking everything except a "white list" or "allow list"; and blocking entire categories such as chat rooms and newsgroups.[3]

Let's look briefly at each of those methods.

Blocking by Address

This method uses a team of filtering company employees to scour the Internet, looking for offensive sites. Sites are selected using one of the categories created by the company. These categories might include "full nudity," "profanity," "drug use," "sex acts," and so on. These are then placed on a "stop list." Many libraries use this kind of blocking. The software is updated frequently because new sites come online every day.

Blocking by Word

A second method is to block sites based on a list of banned words contained in the software. According to

Burt, this is the method used by early filtering systems, and its shortcomings are the reason critics still believe filtering systems are unreliable or ineffective. Word blocking can't be done without also blocking good sites. For example, a banned word like *breast* could block breast cancer information sites.

Blocking Everything Except a "White List" or "Allow List"

This method, which relies on a preselected list of approved sites, is close to 100 percent effective, says Burt. But it leaves out many useful sites because the reviewers haven't discovered them yet. Burt notes, "While the future holds great potential for such an approach, for now it is only recommended for situations where complete effectiveness in blocking pornography is needed, such as with small children."

Blocking Entire Categories Such as Chat Rooms and Newsgroups

According to Burt, most filters allow the blocking of whole portions of the Internet, such as newsgroups, chat rooms, E-mail, and games. Libraries often use this option

A Shocking Example

In testimony before a committee of the U.S. Congress, Dr. Mark Laaser said, "Pornography that is violent in nature is certainly available in a variety of forms. The other day, in preparing for my testimony, I pulled up a[n Internet browser] menu that included 25 forms of sadomasochistic activity, including blood-letting, … and I got into it in less than 60 seconds."[4]

because they don't feel it is good use of computer time for individuals to be talking away in chat rooms when others might be waiting to do real research on the Web.

What Choices Do You Have For Filtering?

Steve Watters, Internet research analyst at Focus on the Family, has done extensive research on filtering options. In an article in *Plugged In*, a Focus publication that deals with teens and cultural issues, Watters noted that two-thirds of children ages 2 to 18 have computers at home, and 45 percent of those have Internet access. He also pointed out that there are more than 100 software producers involved in creating family-friendly filtering systems. Which one is right for your family? According to Watters, that depends on your individual needs.[5]

There are basically four different ways to filter pornography and other objectionable materials from your Internet service:

1. *Your Internet browser,* whether Netscape, Microsoft's Internet Explorer, or some other browser, *may* have parental controls installed that allow you to keep your children from accessing sexual or profane materials. Internet Explorer, for example, has a "Content Advisor" you can customize. This feature uses a rating system called RSAC (Recreational Software Advisory Council). To access this, open up Internet Explorer offline and click on the Tools menu. Select Internet Options. Under this,

click on the Content tab. Then click Enable. A new window will pop up, and you'll see a series of categories you can choose from: language, nudity, sex, and violence. Below this window, you'll see a slider bar you can move back and forth with your mouse to determine just how much your children are allowed to see. You highlight the category and then use the bar to make your adjustments. Once you've done that, you then click on the General tab and you'll be given the option of setting up a password to protect your adjustments from tampering. You will then become the "Content Supervisor."

Your Help button can assist you during this process. Or you can purchase a book that explains Internet Explorer's various functions. Once your settings are in place, if your child or anyone else in your family tries to access a porn site, it will be blocked. A window will appear that says, "Sorry, Content Advisor will not allow you to see this site." Only you, as the Content Supervisor, can unlock a blocked site.

2. *Your ISP or search engine* may also provide parental controls or a filtering system. Alta Vista, for example, is both a free Internet service and an incredibly extensive search engine that you can use to find other sites on the Net. This service provides a "Family Filter" that you can turn on or off. Alta Vista has entered into a partnership with SurfWatch, one of the leading filtering software companies in the U.S.

Your ISP may be a local company or a major player like America Online, Prodigy, CompuServe, or Microsoft Network. AOL, Prodigy, and CompuServe all use Cyber

Patrol as their filtering system. As you'll see in a later section, Cyber Patrol is an effective filtering program, but there are some serious moral issues to ponder as you decide if you want to purchase this particular system.

3. *Filtering software* can be installed on your computer. Dozens of programs are available, and they vary in complexity and ease of use.

4. You can use a *Christian or biblically based ISP*. American Family Online, Integrity Online, and other morally based ISPs offer filtering from their sites. In many ways, this can be far more effective than installing a filtering program on your computer, but you may want to strongly consider using *both* to provide maximum protection for your child.

Focus on the Family offers a series of suggestions to help you make an informed decision about what kind of software to buy or ISP to subscribe to[6]:

♦ Examine the price. Many ISPs provide server filtering as a value-added service and therefore offer it for free, or at least at an affordable price.

♦ Test the speed. ISPs that filter their service through a proxy may run a little slower, but some companies have worked to speed up the process.

♦ Examine the filtering focus. Each company has a philosophy for filtering; some have tight filters and others loose. Some companies are even reluctant to disclose their filtering philosophy.

♦ Find out if the service is customizable. Some companies take a "one size fits all" approach and give the same filtered service to every customer. You may want to be able to block more than the company blocks or to override some of the sites that are blocked.

♦ Find out if the service blocks or monitors additional features such as E-mail, chat rooms, or newsgroups. Some server-based filters only monitor the Web and overlook these other dangerous areas of the Internet.

♦ Find out if you can report additional bad sites. Many filtered services "deputize" their customers and encourage them to report questionable sites in order to build their list of blocked sites.

REVIEW YOUR OPTIONS TO MAKE AN INFORMED CHOICE

In Appendix B, we list Web sites that offer current information on computer software programs and ISPs that filter objectionable materials from their mainframe computers. We do not recommend any one ISP or software package, leaving those choices to you, but we do want to mention our concerns about Cyber Patrol.

Cyber Patrol is a Massachusetts-based software filtering company that uses an advisory board to determine which Web sites will be considered off-limits. One of Cyber Patrol's advisors since 1996 is GLAAD, the Gay and Lesbian Alliance Against Defamation. Among Cyber Patrol's forbidden topics is "intolerance" or "hate speech." Through the influence of GLAAD, Cyber Patrol added the antipornography group the American Family Association (AFA) to its list of banned Web sites in 1998. AFA was cited as being "intolerant" of homo-sexuality because it publishes materials opposing the militant gay agenda.

Cyber Patrol is a major player in the internet filter-ing business. As mentioned earlier, it's used by three of the major ISPs: America Online, Prodigy, and Com-puServe (which is owned by AOL). While only 25 per-cent of libraries utilize some degree of filtering, many that do use Cyber Patrol. In effect, profamily Christian groups such as AFA are now considered guilty of "hate speech," and their Web sites are forbidden. This cen-sorship of a biblically based position on homosexuality is alarming. Groups like Focus on the Family, Family Research Council, Traditional Values Coalition, and others fighting the militant homosexual agenda are also considered "intolerant" by GLAAD.

Cyber Patrol is also used by IBM, Bell Atlantic, Netscape, Novell, AT&T, and many more major com-puter and communications companies. Ironically, in 2000, AT&T's cable TV system joined forces with a hard-core pornography company called The Hot Net-work, which features such programs as "Wages of Sin" and "Cheerleader Strippers." Will AT&T's own Web site have to be blocked by Cyber Patrol because it advertises The Hot Network? If you wish to protest AT&T's entrance into the porn business, we'll provide some suggestions in chapter 7.

Another helpful resource for making an informed choice about filtering software and ISPs is the GetNet-Wise Web site (www.getnetwise.org). Sponsored by a group of ISPs and public interest groups, it includes an online safety guide, a list of tools you can use to protect your child, help in reporting online sexual seductions, a listing of Web sites for kids, and much more. One of the most helpful services is a searchable database that allows you to choose what features you would like for your family. You can check a series of features, and the search engine will then find the right product for you. Some of the categories are: software that "limits time" on the Web, filters sex, filters hate, filters violence, and monitors where a child goes on the Internet.

If you'd rather not have a computer in your home but you still want access to the Internet, consider purchasing WebTV. We're not endorsing this product, but it is one option for you. With WebTV, you'll have E-mail accounts, news, sports, and a search engine for surfing the Net. In addition, WebTV uses the Internet filtering system SurfWatch to minimize your child's exposure to pornographic sites. You can also hook up a printer and print hard copies of your E-mails or research findings. WebTV provides an extra safety feature, too; because it's attached to your TV, your Internet access will be in an open area where you can easily monitor where your children are going on the Net.

Fighting Porn Spam

Even if no one in your household ever goes looking for a pornographic Web site, you may still find yourself exposed—thanks to a practice called "porn spam." In Internet jargon, *spam* refers to mass unsolicited E-mailings sent by advertisers to computer users. Pornographers use spam to tempt people to access their Web sites. Their messages usually contain links that a person can click on to go immediately to the porn site. Unsuspecting kids can receive these E-mails because they're sent out indiscriminately.

Depending on the kind of ISP you're using, you may find that the company has a "junk mail" control you can use to block many of these messages. In addition, Morality in Media, one of the oldest antipornography groups in the country (www.moralityinmedia.org), suggests you do the following if you begin receiving porn spam:

1. Don't reply to the message, and don't respond to any removal instructions.

2. Complain to your U.S. attorney's office. Ask them to investigate a possible violation of federal obscenity laws.

3. Complain to your ISP. Most ISPs have policies against spamming.

To report unwanted porn spam, you'll need the pornographer's Internet address, or URL (Uniform Resource Locator). If the address is just a series of numbers instead of words, you can have those numbers translated by going to a Web site called Abuse.net.

Once you have the correct Internet address, you can track down the service provider the pornographer is using by contacting the InterNic Directory. (You can do a word search to find the InterNic site; this group is the official registry of Internet site names.) Once you learn the name of the administrator of the Web site being used by the pornographer, contact the company and complain that you've been spammed.

Besides complaining about spam, you might also consider installing anti-spam software on your computer. It will help you deal with all sorts of junk E-mail messages. Check out the Anti-Spam Resource Center on the Web for more detailed and timely information.

Be aware, too, that hundreds of services on the Internet provide private, free E-mail accounts. Any person—including your child—can subscribe to one (or more) of these E-mail services and receive messages (including porn spam) outside of your regular ISP, in which case you wouldn't even be aware of it.

Hotmail from Microsoft is the largest of these free services, and its users are favorite targets of pornographers. I (Frank) had to close my Hotmail account because I was being routinely spammed by porn marketers. The E-mails usually contained teasers for photos of "sexy teens" or other, more bizarre porn sites, and then provided a link to the porn Web page.

How many 16-year-old boys are self-controlled enough to resist clicking on a link in an E-mail? Fortunately, you can check the history feature on your browser to see if your child has been accessing a secret E-mail account. The history list will show you where he's been, and you can click on any suspicious links to discover what he's been accessing.

CHECKING HISTORY, COOKIES, AND TEMPORARY FILES

Your browser's history section allows you to discreetly find out where your child has been on the Internet during the past few days. At the top of most browsers, you'll find a button that says "History." When you click on that button, a window will pop up on the left side of your screen. In it will be a listing of every Web site you or anyone else has visited on that computer during the past few days.

You may wish to make it a house rule that you and your spouse will review the browser history each week. If someone has gone where he shouldn't, that person will be disciplined appropriately (perhaps a first offender loses Internet privileges for a week, a second offender for a month, etc.).

You can adjust the settings in your history file according to how many days' Internet activity you want to review. Click on the Tools button, then go down to Internet Options. Click on this and you'll see a window pop up. Under History, you'll see a smaller button you can click on that allows you to determine how many days' listings you want saved. For example, if you want to track where your child has been for a month, type 30 or 31 days into the window.

While you're in the Internet Options window, look at the Temporary Files folder. Whenever someone accesses a Web page, an image of that page is saved in this folder, which is inside your Windows programming. You can empty this folder frequently, but you can also go into it to see what your child has viewed. To get to your Temporary Files folder, first click on your Windows folder. Scroll down until you find it. Once inside Temporary Files, you'll see dozens of files listed. Many of them will have names that end in a period, followed by the word "gif". This indicates that it's a type of photo format. You'll also see icons (or logos) that have an "html" at the end. This is a Web page. You must click on these to see the photos or pages.

The Temporary Files folder will contain all sorts of photos you or your child may have accessed on the computer. If you're concerned that your child may be accessing porn sites, you'll also want to check for stored images in other areas of your computer. Photos will have a name plus an extension, which includes a period and a three- or four-letter word (extension) that indicates what kind of file it is. A Microsoft Word file, for example, will have a period and "doc" as the extension. A photo will have one of the following extensions: "gif", "bmp", "tif", or "jpg". Video files may have mpeg, RealG2, Windows Media, Apple Quicktime, AVI, or other extensions. Computer programmers design new video formats or upgrade old formats every few months, so this list is not exhaustive.

To find every photograph on your computer, you can click on your Start button (with a Microsoft logo) on your taskbar at the bottom of your monitor screen. On the menu, then click Find. A window will pop up and ask you what you want to search for. In the Named section, just type the extension. Type in "tif", for example, click Search, and the computer will find every graphic image with a "tif" extension. You can do this with every photo format. For more information about the legal issues involved with these stored images, refer to Appendix A.

In addition, you may wish to check your cookies folder inside the Windows folder. A "cookie" is a small program that many advertisers drop inside your computer if you access their Web pages. It may monitor your purchases, or it may store encoded information such as passwords you use when you buy online. To get to your Windows folder, click on My Computer on your desktop. Then click on your C-Drive folder. Inside that folder, you'll see the Windows folder. Open this folder to locate the cookies folder. This folder can help you determine where your child has gone on the Web.

You'll want to be careful about deleting cookies, especially if you purchase online—you may wipe out your personal information or passwords you need to do business. Therefore, check the name of each cookie carefully before you delete it. If you open up a cookie, you'll just find coding. The name on the file, however, can give you a sense of where it came from.

COMPUTER PASSWORDS

If you have a particular reason for concern that your child may be tempted by online pornography, you can take the extra step of instituting a password system on the computer he uses in your home. You can set it up so that only you or your spouse are permitted to log on. If your child wants to use the computer, you'll have to log on for him. This way, he can't access porn sites (or anything else) after you've gone to bed or while you're out of the house.

Obviously, using such a system can sometimes be an inconvenience for both you and your child. It might also prompt accusatory questions like "Why don't you trust me? What did I do to deserve this?" Thus, you don't want to rush into installing this kind of system. However, if you know your child has gone looking for porn in any form before, or is just too immature to use even a filtered Internet unsupervised, it may be a necessary precaution that's worth the hassle.

STAYING INFORMED

Things change so rapidly on the Internet that it's easy to feel overwhelmed at the thought of pornography invading your home this way. To help you, we've provided an extensive list of reliable resources at the end of this book, but there are several key organizations that can keep you well-informed on the pornography issue. Each of these has Web sites and automated E-mail services so you can be updated frequently.

The first, of course, is Focus on the Family and its PureIntimacy Web site. Second, access resources from the Family Research Council (FRC). Jan LaRue is FRC's senior director of legal studies and publishes a weekly E-mail newsletter titled *Legal Facts* that deals with pornography and other threats to the family. Third, the American Family Association (AFA) offers a wealth of information on the devastating consequences of pornography. Fourth, Enough Is Enough! is a good resource on this topic. Fifth, use the resources provided by Citizens for Community Values, a Cincinnati-based group that has taken a major leadership role in fighting pornography and homosexual activism. Sixth, check out Morality in Media's Web site for well-researched information on obscenity and pornography. We'll list dozens more at the end of this book, but you can begin with these.

SEEKING GOD'S HELP

This entire chapter has been about what you can do as a parent to keep porn out of your home. As you've seen, there's a lot to think about and a lot you can do. But let's never lose sight of the fact that in this area, as in every other area of life, the first and best thing we can do is to seek God's help through prayer. He is the ultimate source of the wisdom we need as parents, and He also knows the heart and the actions of every member of your family.

Thus, as you and your spouse (if you're married) begin to make plans to protect your home from porn, start on your knees, asking for His wisdom and guidance. Remember that He loves your child and wants him or her to stay pure even more than you do. And as you start to implement your plans, continue to seek His wisdom and strength for the task day by day. He *will* provide.

"If any of you lacks wisdom, he should ask God, who gives generously to all without finding fault, and it will be given to him" (James 1:5).

CHAPTER SEVEN

How to Oppose Pornography in Your Community

Nashville, Tennessee, the center of a thriving metropolis of more than a million people, is known as the buckle on America's Bible Belt. It's home to the headquarters of the Southern Baptist Convention, more than 600 churches, and numerous Christian publishing houses, recording companies, colleges, and other ministries.

It also has more porn outlets (strip clubs and adult bookstores) per capita than any other city in the country, including New York and Los Angeles.

Significantly, Sexaholics Anonymous moved its national headquarters to Nashville recently, and at least two antipornography groups are considering Nashville as a target for a major campaign at the time of this writing. In the early 1990s, Christians tried to launch a movement against porn there, but it fizzled out as quickly as it began.

According to one profamily leader, Nashville passed a poorly written zoning law several years ago that has had the effect of actually *helping* the pornographers. A local TV station did a special investigative report on the blight of porn in Nashville and found that pornographers from out of state have flocked into town because they know the city is wide open to them.

We tell you all this about Nashville because it illustrates that any community, even those we might least expect, can be inundated with porn unless concerned individuals take the threat seriously and act together to stop it. That's why we encourage you, once you've established safeguards in your home and are determined to remain vigilant to protect your child, to expand your efforts to include your community. Do everything you can to make your city safer for all its children, including yours.

TAKE IT TO THE CHURCH

In thinking about working to make your town more safe from the harm done by porn, we suggest you look first at your own church. Just as Nashville might be a surprising city to have a porn problem, so you might also assume people in your church are unlikely to be struggling with porn. But the reality is that there may be as many as 10 to 20 percent of your church membership who wrestle with a pornography addiction. This includes pastors. This hidden scourge will only grow worse if it's not discussed openly.

Here are some recent statistics:

• Dr. Harry Schaumburg, in *False Intimacy*, quotes from a *Leadership* magazine survey of 300 pastors that 23 percent admitted they had done something sexual with someone other than their spouse. Twelve percent admitted to having sexual intercourse outside of marriage.

• At one Promise Keepers men's event, 50 percent of the attendees admitted to dabbling in porn during the previous week.

• Dr. Mark Laaser estimates that 10 percent of Christian men are sexually addicted or compulsive in their sexual behaviors (National Coalition for the Protection of Children & Families data).

• Roger Charman of Focus on the Family's Pastoral Ministries says that about 20 percent of the calls on their pastoral care line are for help with issues such as pornography and compulsive behavior.

• One researcher estimates that 60 million Americans have visited sexually explicit Web sites. Tragically, the percentage of Christian men involved is not much different from that of the unsaved. According to another survey of pastors and lay leaders conducted by *Leadership* magazine, 62 percent have regularly viewed pornography.[1]

♦ Ted Roberts, a pastor who provides counseling for sex addicts, conducted a survey among the pastors he knows. He found that 21 to 29 percent of them were what he would call "sexually addicted."

My wife and I (Frank) know a married couple who started a ministry to sex addicts in our church eight years ago. The husband had been introduced to porn by his own mother in a misguided effort to teach him how to be a man. His father was involved in pornography and never overcame it, even to his dying day. This couple put a small notice in the church bulletin and found themselves overwhelmed by the response from church members.

The man began meeting weekly with the sex-addicted husbands; his wife met with their wives. They dealt with a pastor who had become AIDS-infected and eventually died. Another counselee was a pastor who had been caught having sex with a little boy. His wife eventually divorced him. Others were heavily addicted to pornography.

Within four months, this couple was emotionally drained from the intensity of the ministry and the spiritual warfare surrounding it. Eventually, they had to give it up. (At that time, there were few resources available for counseling sex addicts. However, as the problem has grown, so have the number of therapists and books on the subject. Today, this couple would have good resources and support groups to aid them.)

How might you help to address the problem of porn in and through your church? We suggest four possibilities, beginning with ministering to those who struggle.

Start a ministry to porn addicts. Sex addicts need to know that they can get the help they need from people who are willing to pray for them and hold them accountable. So one of the first things you might consider is establishing a "Faithful & True" ministry in your church. Dr. Laaser and Rob Jackson pioneered this effort. The Faithful & True ministry is based on the Alcoholics Anonymous 12-step program. You'll find contact information for Jackson's and Laaser's groups in the resource section of this book.

If you're not comfortable starting such a ministry in your own church, check out the Faithful & True Web site to see if there's already a chapter in your city (www.faithfulandtrueministries.com). This is an essential step to take if you're serious about fighting pornography in your community. There's no point in trying to rescue people from this addictive behavior if there's no follow-up or support to help keep them free. Leading a man to Christ in front of an adult bookstore will save his soul from hell, but it may not result in his deliverance from such a serious addiction. God can deliver someone instantly from this sin, but more frequently it occurs over time.

Prayerfully consider starting a sex addicts ministry in your church. If you do start one, you'll probably be shocked at the number of individuals who come forward for help.

Start a ministry to wives of porn addicts. You may also want to consider getting involved in Esther Ministries, an outreach to women whose husbands are porn addicted. This group has a helpful Web site, conducts workshops, and has a newsletter. Check the ministry out at www.estheronline.org.

Start a ministry to girls in strip clubs. Amy Dupree is a former strip club dancer who became a Christian several years ago. Her ministry, Amy's Friends, now helps other women trapped in the strip club scene. Says Dupree on her Web site, "The only goal of this ministry is to change the lives of women who are in the adult entertainment business and sincerely want to leave.... Desiring a better life, they are often without a high school diploma, vocational training, workplace-appropriate clothing and/or job interview skills. They are trapped in the darkness of this industry." Her ministry helps them get their GED, job training, suitable clothing, interview skills, subsidized housing, and health care while they rebuild their lives.

You can start a local Amy's Friends in your community. The group has a detailed workbook online to show you how. To learn more about Amy's Friends, access its Web site at www.amysfriends.org, or see Appendix B for address and phone number.

Challenge the porn pushers. My wife and I (Frank) have been involved in a new effort at our church to deal with the pornography plague here in Nashville. Our small group meets each week to pray and become better informed about the nature of the porn industry. We take a church bus to an adult bookstore once or twice a month. We park across the street from the store and set up a table with coffee and donuts, hoping that someone will cross the street to talk to us. We pray for everyone going into the store, and we have sexual addiction resources available for anyone who's interested.

Prior to our becoming involved in this outreach, the young man who spearheaded the bookstore effort said he'd seen one man commit his life to Christ. Another man came across the street and confided, "Will you pray for me? I'm not supposed to be here." He was a regular churchgoer.

We'll say more about this kind of direct action later in the chapter.

TAKE IT TO NEIGHBORS AND FRIENDS

For your child's sake, it's not enough to keep your own home free of pornography. Unless you forbid him to

---

Fight Back!

Activist parents who work with the American Decency Association in Indiana won a significant victory over Howard Stern's pornographic and anti-Christian radio program. In April 2000, Indianapolis radio station WNAP dropped Stern from its lineup. The *Indianapolis Star* reported on April 5, "Stern was difficult to sell to advertisers, who were pressured to pull their commercials by people who thought the show was vulgar. It takes guts for an advertiser to stand up to the public pressure, and most businesses want to avoid any controversy." This victory was due to moms and dads getting together with the help of the American Decency Association to contact advertisers about their sponsorship of Stern. There's one less moral polluter in Indiana today because of citizen activism.

leave the house, he is going out into a sex-saturated culture every day. As we've noted in earlier chapters, his
friends may be accessing porn on the Internet or viewing pornographic movies while their parents are at
work. If your child sleeps over at a friend's house, they
may be staying up late to view porn. In short, despite
your best efforts to block pornography out of your own
home, your child may get it elsewhere.

If you haven't already done so, strongly consider
talking to your neighbors and friends about the dangers
of porn. Find out if friends' and neighbors' homes where
your child spends time have computers with unfiltered
Internet access.

◆ Do those parents know what their children are
viewing?

◆ Teach them how to check the browser history feature to find out what their kids are viewing. Are they
willing to establish ground rules for Internet use with
their own children?

◆ Do those families subscribe to premium movie
channels, including those with sexual content?

◆ Are they aware of what sexually explicit films
their cable or satellite service is offering? Are their children allowed to watch whatever they wish?

◆ Do those neighbors and friends and their spouses
work outside the home, leaving their children home
alone and unmonitored every weekday? If your child is
spending time there while the parents are away, what
are the kids doing? One rule you might set is that your
child is only allowed in homes where at least one parent is present.

The discussion you have with your neighbors and friends may seem awkward, but it's much needed. Some may think you're overreacting or simply a prude for wanting to protect your child from pornographic materials. Don't allow them to dissuade you from doing what's right. You may actually be forced in some circumstances to cut off all contact with a neighbor or friend over this issue. In the long run, however, what's more important, their approval or being a good parent by protecting your child? If they're ignorant about the dangers of porn (as most people are), and if they're open to new information, consider giving them a copy of this book.

Counting the Cost and Making Strategic Plans

If you're feeling that the Lord would have you get involved beyond your neighborhood, confronting the plague of porn in your community, please count the cost and pray before you get started. Those who have taken on this challenge have discovered that they're not only dealing with spiritual forces, but also with very real earthly forces that are well organized and have millions of dollars at their disposal to fight any opposition.

Be prepared to be misquoted or ridiculed in the local newspaper. You may receive subtle legal threats from the American Civil Liberties Union. (If you face such threats, rest assured that groups like the American Family Association [AFA], the National Law Center for

Children and Families, Morality in Media [MIM], or other antiporn groups will be there to provide you with excellent legal advice.)

The reality is that you will probably find only a few individuals willing to stand with you in this battle. You may be ignored or even maligned within your own church. Many Christians prefer comfort to confrontation; they want to be "nice" rather than to be right or to challenge evil within their communities. There is no way to sugarcoat this issue. You will be facing evil, and you must expect opposition—both within the church and outside it.

If, after prayerfully considering all that, you're willing to pay the price, then take your stand!

Assuming you have found at least a small group of fellow churchgoers who share your concerns about pornography's impact on your community, the next step is to begin planning which pornography outlets you will go after first. Each community is different, of course. There are any number of potential targets. They include the following: adult arcades; adult book, novelty, or video stores; adult night clubs, gentlemen's clubs, or strip bars; adult motels or hotels; adult theaters; escort agencies; massage parlors; nude modeling studios; sexual encounter centers. We must also include public and school libraries with unfiltered Internet access. Further, your city may not have laws governing the display of pornographic magazines in bookstores, grocery stores, and newsstands. If it doesn't, you can push for a law that will require porn magazines to have a cover placed in front of them—and out of reach of children.

Where you begin depends on the seriousness of the particular threat in your community. Your area may have problems with adult bookstores but not massage parlors, or vice versa. You may have good laws on the books, but they're not being enforced. You'll need to research these things in your local library or through your police vice squad or city attorney to discover what your city officials are doing about pornography. A good law that's not enforced is useless.

As you start confronting pornography in your community, you may want to become affiliated with a national antiporn group. Several have local or state chapters. These can provide your church group with a sense of identity and national support. The AFA, for example, has state and local chapters. Citizens for Community Values (CCV), an excellent group based in Cincinnati, uses local volunteers. MIM, one of the oldest antiporn groups in the U.S., has information on its Web site showing how to start a local chapter. Each of these groups offers a wealth of information, including videos, books, pamphlets, billboards, and more, to help you in your efforts.

Most antiporn groups, like FRC and MIM, have Web sites filled with helpful advice and searchable databases for information on pornography. Some, like the AFA's Law Center, the National Law Center, MIM, and the Community Defense Counsel, provide legal advice and help in crafting effective antiporn laws.

In any effort of this kind, we can't overemphasize the importance of prayer. Every person involved in this ministry should be praying and should have others praying for him. Getting involved in this issue means

---

Two Sisters Turn Their Pain into Power

Gail Bowen and Shelley Timmermeier have much more in common than simply being sisters. Both of them and their mother were repeatedly molested by a close relative, though none of them knew the others were being molested until years later, when the relative was caught trying to assault the mother. The man had been a pornography addict who was acting out his sexual fantasies on his female relatives. When the truth came to the surface, they had to undergo long-term therapy to work through the trauma of being violated by someone they had trusted.

Gail and Shelley, however, are turning their pain into power. They've linked arms with the Salvation Army and Morality in Media to conduct yearly "Pornography Awareness Weeks" in their community. They've convinced stores to put porn magazines behind covered racks to keep them away from children. They're now starting a campaign to get filtering systems on all library computers.

Gail has some helpful advice for those getting involved in fighting pornography: "You have a big fight on your hands, but the goal is to educate people. You need to let people know that if they don't fight it, they're accepting it. You have to take a stand one way or another." Shelley notes, "I'm still in counseling after all these years, but it gives me the strength to fight it. If I can save one person, one child, from being beaten or feeling like he's nothing, then it's worth fighting for."

entering into spiritual warfare, and there may be casualties if you're not continually praying for protection. Pornography is one of Satan's key strongholds, and he will not give up territory without a fight. We're not encouraging paranoia but a realistic view of what's involved in this battle.

To protect our antiporn group at my (Frank's) church, each of us has enlisted two people to pray for us each week.

TAKE IT TO THE CITY/STATE/FEDERAL GOVERNMENTS

As you prayerfully consider taking on the pornography plague in your community, you need to be aware of a concept called "community standards." The phrase "community standards" comes from *Miller v. California* (413 U.S. 15), a key Supreme Court case decided in 1973 that defines what "obscenity" is for judges, prosecutors, and juries. In this decision, the Court said that for a jury to decide whether something is obscene, the material has to be judged by community standards—not by a national standard. The Court said, "It is not realistic nor constitutionally sound to read the First Amendment as requiring that the people of Maine or Mississippi accept public depiction of conduct found tolerable in Las Vegas or New York City."

The way a city or area can establish its own community standard is to bring obscenity lawsuits against those distributing pornographic materials. The jury then decides what is obscene, based on its understanding and interpretation of the legal definition of obscenity given by the Supreme Court. The AFA's publication *A Guide to What One Person Can Do About Pornography* notes, "The best way to firmly establish community standards is through consistent enforcement of the obscenity laws. Businesses that distribute sexually oriented material will clearly see the types of material that will be accepted by the community and those that will not. Communities like Cincinnati, Ohio, that have eliminated the distribution of obscene material have done so in large part because of consistent law enforcement efforts. This model can be replicated in any community, and every community can maintain an environment free of illegal obscene material."

CCV has taken a leadership role in keeping its city porn free. The keys are consistency and persistence in filing lawsuits against pornographers. According to CCV head Phil Burress, "The key phrase is 'Silence is acceptance.' If you see something you believe to be obscene and you are silent, you are, in reality, accepting it as a community standard." Until there's vigorous prosecution, a city or area will not have a high community standard of what it will accept.

A number of laws are available for use in fighting porn. Many communities and states have good laws on the books, but it bears repeating that they have to be enforced to do any good. Your community may be flooded with pornographic materials, yet you could have a prosecutor who doesn't care about the issue or is uninformed about the dangers of porn.

Local/State Laws

Listed below are local and state laws that are typically used to combat porn or to protect children from exposure to pornographic materials:

• *Harmful to Minor Statutes:* These laws make it illegal to sell, exhibit, or display harmful (soft-core) pornography to minor children, even if the material is not obscene or illegal for adults. Examples of violations are: displaying, selling, or renting pornography or other sexually explicit material to a minor.

• *Sexually Oriented Businesses (SOBs):* An SOB can be a strip club, massage parlor, adult bookstore, or theater. These can be regulated by the city or state in two major ways: (1) A community can pass zoning regulations controlling where SOBs are located. (2) Licensing requirements can force SOB employees to undergo stringent background checks for criminal records, as well as regulate the time and hours of operation and what kinds of activities can take place on the premises. A licensing law can also require SOBs to comply with all health and safety laws and those prohibiting prostitution or pandering. In addition, a licensing law can require that doors be removed from peep show booths to reduce the incidence of masturbation and the spread of sexually transmitted diseases.

Keep in mind that you can't legally close an SOB unless it is violating state health codes, obscenity laws, nuisance laws, and so on. What a city can do, however, is control what are called the "secondary effects" of a pornography business. These include such things as: increased crime, decreased property values, increased social blight, sexually transmitted diseases, and so on. The National Law Center for Children and Families has a legal manual on how your city can enact an effective law regulating SOBs. The Community Defense Counsel (CDC) also has a manual called *Protecting Communities from Sexually Oriented Businesses.* This 400-page volume will guide the community activist and city prosecutor through the maze of legal landmines to craft a law that can limit the damage SOBs can do to your community. Check CDC's Web site for details: www.communitydefense.org.

What if your local prosecutors won't go after pornographers? If you suspect a video or magazine is legally obscene, have two people rent or purchase the material. Get a receipt with the store name, date, time, and video or magazine title on it. Make a copy of the receipt before turning the material over to the authorities.

This tactic is most effective if you know that this material has already been deemed legally obscene in another state. If it has, chances are better that it will also be ruled obscene in your state. Antiporn groups can help you determine this.

If law enforcement officials still refuse to act, you may have to swear out a complaint against the porn dealer. Then the officials will be forced to act. Another option is to take the material to the district attorney and ask for a grand jury to review it. Public pressure is another way to get officials to prosecute. Many law enforcement officials are elected, and the ballot box can remove those who are unwilling to uphold the laws against obscenity. There are half a dozen antiporn law groups that will be more than happy to help you go after pornographers in your town (see Parent's Rights Groups/Legal Defense in the resources appendix).

Federal Laws

The federal government has authority to regulate and prosecute the distribution of illegal materials. Federal authorities have oversight in the following areas:

◆ *Obscenity laws.* There's a difference between pornography and material that is legally obscene. Nonobscene porn is protected by the First Amendment. Obscene material and child porn are not protected and can be prosecuted. Federal prosecutors have authority over the distribution of pornography via the U.S. mail, buses, trains, planes, UPS, and so on. During the Clinton/Gore Administration, federal prosecution of pornography hit an all-time low. (For more about this, see Appendix A.)

◆ *Indecent materials on TV and radio.* The Federal Communications Commission (FCC) has authority to bring charges against stations for broadcasting indecent materials. It does not, however, monitor what's aired. That job belongs to listeners, who must file charges if they believe something is indecent. The FCC has a stringent set of requirements for listeners who file complaints.

According to the AFA, if you hear something on the radio that you believe is illegal, your complaint must include the following: (1) name, time, and date of a specific program or advertisement; (2) a narrative of the complaint, including a tape or transcript of the program or significant excerpts; and (3) the call sign of the station involved, radio frequency or TV station channel, with city and state. To file a complaint, write to the FCC, Complaints and Political Programming Branch, 2025 M Street, NW, Room 8210, Enforcement Division, Mass Media Bureau, Washington, D.C. 20554; fax: 202-418-1124; E-mail: complaints-enf@fcc.gov.

• *Transmission of obscene materials by Internet, phone, mail, or transport.* If you receive obscene or sexually explicit materials through the mail, you can file a complaint with the post office. You can also fill out Postal Form 1500 and send it to the pornographer. This will direct him to stop sending you sexually explicit materials. If he continues, he can be fined. If your minor child is involved in dial-a-porn calls, you can file charges against the dial-a-porn business for providing pornography to a minor. If you discover child porn on your computer or receive such materials in the mail, you can immediately file a complaint with the U.S. Justice Department. Child porn is against the law, period. There does not need to be proof of obscenity for it to be prosecuted. File your complaint with the Child Exploitation and Obscenity Section, U.S. Justice Dept., Criminal Division, 1001 G Street, NW, Washington, D.C. 20530.

Take It to the Library

Thanks in large measure to the efforts of the American Library Association (ALA), local libraries are being converted into adult bookstores and peep show booths— and you're footing the bill for it. As we noted in an earlier chapter, the ALA contends that unlimited "access to information" is a constitutional right that extends to minors. The ALA's "Library Bill of Rights," which has no legal authority, is treated as binding by many libraries, thus creating a situation where library computers are mostly unfiltered and pornography is easily accessible.

Recently, the ALA held workshops to discuss how libraries should begin carrying "erotica" collections as well as prohomosexual materials. These materials will be freely available to your child. In addition, because of the ALA's belief in the "right to privacy" of every patron, you will not be permitted to know what kinds of materials your child is checking out. In the ALA's view, your child's "privacy right" supersedes your parental rights.

In response to the arrogance of the ALA in usurping local control of the library system and your parental rights, former librarian Karen Jo Gounaud founded Family Friendly Libraries (FFL) several years ago. Her goal is to educate parents on their rights as taxpayers to control the policies of local libraries. She also strives to educate librarians on their rights and responsibilities to serve the public—not the political interests of the ALA.

On her FFL Web site (www.fflibraries.org),

Gounaud provides parents and librarians with a wealth of information on the dangers of unfiltered computers and the liberal political agenda of the ALA. She also gives the reader sensible solutions to help libraries become family friendly again.

FFL believes that libraries should enact the following: (1) more commonsense policies to protect children from exposure to age-inappropriate materials without parental consent; and (2) return to policies placing libraries under maximum local control, with more acknowledgment of taxpayer authority and community standards.

FFL does not endorse censorship or encourage the removal of materials from the library. But it does oppose the authoritarian control of the ALA over local library policies and practices, especially when those policies violate parental rights and community standards. If you'd like to see local control returned to your public library, consider getting involved in FFL's educational activities.

What steps can you take to find out if your library is family friendly? Gounaud suggests you ask the following questions:

- What is the most direct governing body for your library system?
- How is this governing body put together?
- Who is on the board?
- What is the main document setting day-to-day library policies?
- What is the philosophy behind the policy document?

◆ What procedures are in place for altering or amending library policy?

◆ What policies are in place that affect family life? For example, what rules govern a child's access to Internet pornography?

◆ What are the professional and training requirements of library personnel? What character requirements are sought?

◆ What procedures are in place for filing complaints?

◆ Does the ALA have an influence over spending policies?

◆ Can citizens give input on library book purchases? How are donations handled?

◆ What state and local laws are in place governing sexual activities in a library?

◆ What laws are in effect to protect children from harmful materials?

These are just a sampling of the questions to ask as you investigate your library's policies on pornography and children. See the FFL Web site for more, or order Gounaud's booklet "How to Make Your Library Family Friendly" from FRC at 800/225-4008.

Gounaud lists several areas of conflict between parents and librarians. These include: (1) unaccompanied minors using libraries; (2) minors' right to privacy; (3) controversial sexual themes in children's books; (4) profanity and sexually explicit or suggestive content in books selected for children and youth; (5) children's access to adult materials; (6) pornography on library computer terminals.

Most of these problems would be easily resolved if it weren't for the influence of the ALA over local library policies. As Gounaud observes, "Families with borrowing cards at ALA-minded library systems can't even count on the librarians' cooperation in monitoring their own children's reading. The ALA discourages any policy that will tell an inquiring parent what is currently checked out on their minor child's card. But they are held responsible for the fines on damaged, lost, or overdue books.

"Even when a parent is constantly with a minor child, the children's book sections mix standard kiddie lit with sexually and violently explicit material for 'young adults' that is peppered with profanity. An award winning book is not necessarily a safe choice, either. The ALA controls most of the awards, too. Even kids' picture books often include copies of *Daddy's Roommate*, a gay rights preschool publication. *Boys and Sex*, a sex education book 'for 10 and up' by Wardell Pomeroy (an Alfred Kinsey research partner), even has a written section encouraging kids to secretly consider sex with their pets as a normal activity."

Gounaud warns parents about getting involved in a fight with their local ALA-controlled library. She notes, "Be prepared for a long siege if yours is an entrenched ALA system. Citizens for the past 30 years have allowed that organization's ideology to have a monopolistic influence on most of our nation's libraries. It will not be changed in a matter of days or months."

She also urges parents to avoid treating librarians as

enemies. "Many of them have concerns, too, about exposing children to inappropriate materials, but they hesitate to take strong stands within their liberal professional networks. The library trustees, whether elected or appointed, are supposed to be the official citizens' advocates. They are also highly influenced by the ALA."

Gounaud asks, "Should you let your pre-adolescent or teenager go to the library alone?" Her answer? "My kids are adults now, but if they were younger, I wouldn't send them into our system by themselves—at least not until the influence of the ALA's extremist policies has been cleaned from our system and replaced with responsible and reasonable attitudes."

In addition to working to change antiparent and pro-porn policies within your public library, Gounaud suggests a positive approach. She has launched a "Family Friendly Library Books Week," to be held the same week that the ALA holds its annual "Banned Books Week." She suggests parents check the library's collection of profamily materials to see if there's an imbalance of books from one particular point of view (liberal). If you find a lack of profamily resources or an imbalance, send your librarian a polite letter with a list of possible book selections to be added.

If the librarian refuses to order any of your suggestions, find out what the library's policy is on accepting donated books. If it's permissible, purchase the books yourself or with a group of friends and donate them to the library. Then monitor them to make sure they stay on the shelves. Frequently, profamily books, especially books dealing with pornography, abortion, or homosexuality, have a tendency to disappear or to be vandalized.

Some excellent first choices to donate to your library would be: *Protecting Your Child in an X-Rated World; False Intimacy,* by Dr. Harry Schaumburg; *Talking to Your Kids About Sex,* by Dr. Mark Laaser; *The Silent War: Ministering to Those Trapped in the Deception of Pornography,* by Henry J. Rogers; the *Parents' Guide to the Spiritual Growth of Children,* edited by Dr. John Trent, Rick Osborne, and Kurt Bruner (Focus on the Family/Tyndale); and the *Parents' Guide to the Spiritual Mentoring of Teens,* edited by Joe White and Jim Weidmann (also Focus on the Family/Tyndale). Use the resource list at the back of this book to access organizational Web sites for additional book choices. Each of the groups listed will likely have book recommendations.

Check out the FFL Web site for updates and more ideas about how you can influence your local library system.

If you'd like to take on the issue of Internet pornography on unfiltered computers, you might want to download a copy of the National Law Center for Children and Families' "Internet Use Policy for Libraries." It's available for free at: www.NationalLawCenter.org.

You may wish to read the Family Research Council's report "Dangerous Access." Unfortunately, libraries are becoming hangouts for child molesters who sexually excite themselves and sometimes assault children or other patrons after viewing porn for hours on library computers.

You may also have an opportunity to work with librarians who are fearful of laboring in a hostile office environment. Numerous laws protect women from being forced to work in situations where they feel personally threatened or sexually harassed. You may find a number of librarians who are willing to file class-action lawsuits against the library and city for creating such an environment with unfiltered computers. If polite entreaties about installing filtering systems fail, a threatened lawsuit might do the trick.

"Employers beware," says the AFA, "Title VII of the Civil Rights Act guarantees employees freedom from workplace sexual harassment. Sexual harassment includes situations where employers fail to eliminate hostile work conditions. Hostile work conditions may exist when pornography is pervasively viewed in the workplace. Under the Civil Rights Act, employers are liable for damages if they know, or should have known about hostile work conditions, yet failed to promptly rectify them."

In addition, as you research harmful to minors statutes in your community, you may discover that your library is violating state law by exposing children to Internet porn. A threatened lawsuit based on that violation might also provoke action from librarians.

TAKE IT TO THE STORES

Another area of concern in working to rid your community of pornographic materials is what's available in local stores. If you conduct an informal survey, you might find that grocery stores, mini-marts, bookstores, newsstands, and drug stores are selling pornographic magazines. Regular video stores may be renting pornographic videos—not just mainstream, R-rated films that may contain some nudity but films that are unabashedly and unmistakably porn. Smaller video stores may have back rooms where hard-core videos are available. Many of these may be legally obscene.

Do your homework before approaching a store manager about the pornography he's selling or renting. Find out what laws govern the public display of pornographic materials in your community. Bring statistics with you about the harm done by porn, or purchase copies of MIM's special report *Pornography's Effects on Adults & Children* and give one to each store manager you visit. Don't go alone, either. Take a friend along who can provide moral support. The Lord never sent out His disciples alone but sent them two by two for mutual protection and prayer support.

If you're uncomfortable with a face-to-face encounter with a store manager, write a letter outlining your concerns and requesting that he remove pornography from his store. The AFA has a brief sample letter you can use as a model. It simply states:

> *Dear Manager,*
> *While shopping in your store recently, I could not help but notice that you sell (rent) pornographic magazines (videos). Perhaps you have not consid-*

ered the potential harm such materials have on our community.

Pornography fuels sexual crimes against women and children. Rapists regularly admit to this fact. Statistics also show the largest consumers of pornography are children between the ages of 12 and 17 — some of the most important and formative years of a young person's emotional and sexual development. Pornography is certainly not an appropriate textbook.

Please consider replacing these materials with something more decent and responsible. Until then, my family and I will do business elsewhere and will encourage others to do the same.

Sincerely,

The AFA's *A Guide to What One Person Can Do About Pornography* includes this and more advice on the topic. Check its Web site for ordering information.

TAKE IT TO THE STREETS

If your polite letters and cordial meetings with store managers fail to get them to stop distributing pornography, your next step is to prayerfully consider launching a boycott and/or a picket of the store.

Boycotts and pickets may still be controversial among Christians, but they're legitimate tools to use in putting pressure on businesses that are engaged in antifamily or anti-Christian activities. AFA founder

Donald Wildmon has long advocated boycotts and pickets to change pro-porn corporate policies. After a lengthy boycott of 7-Eleven stores, the AFA was successful in getting the owner (the Southland Corporation) to remove porn magazines from its stores.

The key to winning a boycott is to stick with it for the long haul. It can take five years or more to cause a company enough economic hardship and bad publicity to get it to change its policies. Unfortunately, the only thing many corporations understand is their bottom line; morality or "doing the right thing" often isn't a

---

One Call Changed an Oil Company's Policy on Pornography!

Sometimes it takes only a phone call to make a difference in a community. Arlene Sawicki, an antiporn activist in Chicago with the Archdiocesan Council of Catholic Women, learned how effective one call can be. Several years ago, Arlene walked into a new Shell gas station and mini-mart that had opened in her neighborhood. As she paid her bill, she noticed a rack of soft- and hard-core pornography magazines right next to the door. She didn't say anything to the lady at the register but went right home and called the Shell regional office to file a complaint.

The customer service representative graciously took down her complaint and then visited the station the next day. He called Arlene back immediately and agreed that the magazines were highly offensive. He then called the station franchise owner and gave him two options: Put the magazines behind the counter or get rid of them. The owner chose to remove them immediately.

According to Arlene, the customer service representative called her back two months later and said that he'd informed

consideration. If they're losing money because of a boycott or picket, however, they'll change their policies.

Several years ago, a number of profamily groups, including Focus on the Family, the AFA, and the Southern Baptist Convention (SBC), launched a boycott of the Disney company for its prohomosexual policies and its production of pornographic and blasphemous films. The boycott has not yet brought Disney to its knees, but it has definitely affected its bottom line.

In 1998, I (Frank) wrote a book with Dr. Richard Land, head of the SBC's Ethics and Religious Liberty

---

the Shell corporate office about the obscene magazines. Shell executives had decided to put a clause in all future franchise contracts forbidding the stocking of pornographic magazines! Says Arlene, "When I tell this story, I always say 'See what one phone call can do?' And a big thanks to the agent who was sensitive to his company's integrity and image."

After her positive experience with Shell, Arlene visited a Crown bookstore and saw a young boy pull a pornography magazine from the shelves and head to the back of the store. She reported the incident to the managers, who gave her a speech about the First Amendment. She said she was calling the police, and an officer came to the store to see if Crown was violating any "harmful to minor" statutes. The store now has placed the porn magazines out of the reach of children. In addition, Crown has established a national policy on properly disposing of old porn magazines; they will be placed in locked Dumpsters so children can't find them. These major victories against pornography were achieved because one woman had the courage to confront the system.

Commission, called *Send a Message to Mickey*. It describes the SBC's involvement in the Disney boycott, explains Disney's prohomosexual and pro-porn policies, and discusses the importance of boycotts in bringing about positive social change. Portions of the chapter "Answers to Objections about Boycotting" are excerpted below for your use in your own boycotting efforts:

> OBJECTION: Boycotts don't work.
> FACT: Boycotts do work. But they take time and determination. It can take from five to ten years for a boycott to have its intended effect, according to Todd Putnam, editor of the *National Boycott News*. There are seldom quick victories because the corporation being boycotted figures that its unhappy customers will eventually just give up and start buying its products again. Commitment and persistence are the keys to victory.
> OBJECTION: We should support the good and boycott the bad.
> FACT: If a "family-friendly" restaurant is serving good food to you and your family but is also showing pornographic movies to children in the back room, do you continue visiting the restaurant? Do you "boycott" the back room while still giving money to the restaurant so it can continue to fund its back room activities? By supporting Disney's good films, you're also helping fund Miramax's movies promoting homosexuality, incest, and

pornography. Every dime you give to Disney helps fuel its aggressive prohomosexual agenda.

OBJECTION: A boycott isn't Christian.

FACT: Is it more Christian to give your money to an organization that is anti-Christian? The AFA published an excellent article on this topic, and it's posted on the Internet (http:www.afa.net/index). The issue, says AFA, is one of stewardship and holiness. "The Lord Jesus characterized His followers as stewards, or managers, of all that He gives them, calling them to dispense these resources—including their money—on His behalf and in a responsible manner." How are you spending the money the Lord has given you? Are you spending it on things that please Him or that bring shame to His name?

AFA Journal news editor Ed Vitagliano notes: "Christian responsibility in a fallen world and in an often hostile culture is expressed by at least two well-known New Testament symbols: The believer is called to be the salt of the earth and the light of the world (Matt. 5:13-16). The follower of Christ is a light in a darkened world first by preaching the gospel (2 Cor. 4:4-6) and second by the good works which the believer performs (Matt. 5:16). In these two ways, God's truth is manifest by both word and deed to point unbelievers to the Savior.

"Salt represents a preserving quality of Christians. In society, the Lord's disciples are to resist the corruption of the world and to add blessing to it.

When Christians cease this function, Jesus said they have lost their flavor and have become worthless to the work of the kingdom."

OBJECTION: Boycotting is censorship.

FACT: Censorship is rightly defined as the act of a government entity restraining a media outlet from publishing or broadcasting something. Boycotting is the nonviolent choice of a person to refuse to spend his money at a particular business. It has been likened to high-visibility counteradvertising. While the businessman is free to advertise his products, the boycotter is free to advertise his refusal to buy those products. That's the beauty of the American system of free enterprise and free speech.

OBJECTION: We're going to cause economic hardship to the people employed in the companies we're boycotting.

FACT: When you purchase a Ford from a local dealership, are you concerned about causing financial hardship among the employees at the local Chrysler dealership? What about the Honda salesman? Do you worry about the employees at Safeway when you prefer to shop at the Piggly Wiggly or Kroger? The truth is, if enough people in town prefer Safeway, the competing grocery may eventually go out of business. People may lose their jobs, but this occurs in a free market society. Are you responsible? Or is this simply a matter of people making free choices in an open society about what is best for themselves and their families? ...

A good company will keep its customers and
gain new ones. A company that cheats its customers or gives them an inferior product will eventually shut down. Back to the analogy of the
restaurant with pornography in the back room:
Wouldn't it be better for that restaurant to shut
down and the good waiters and waitresses to get
other jobs, than for the restaurant to stay in business and destroy children in the back room?[2]

In short, boycotting is a legitimate way of bringing
about positive changes in our culture. Antifamily
groups certainly know how to use boycotts. The militant gay movement, for example, conducted an effective
campaign against Dr. Laura Schlessinger's TV show
produced by Paramount Studios. Activists scared off
Procter & Gamble and other sponsors. Their goal was
to destroy her chances of getting on the air with her
profamily message. Why? Because she views homosexual conduct as a moral perversion. Christians could
have launched (but didn't) a counter "buycott" to purchase the products of sponsors who indicated a willingness to stick with Dr. Laura through the controversy.
(Her TV show did get on the air, but it was short-lived
for a number of reasons.)

If you're launching a boycott, you'll want to use the
AFA's considerable expertise on this topic. In addition,
the AFA has developed strategies for conducting pickets of stores that sell pornographic materials.

In *A Guide to What One Person Can Do About*

Pornography, the AFA lays out a simple strategy for conducting a peaceful picket. *The first step* is to visit the store in question to see if it sells magazines like *Playboy, Penthouse,* or *Hustler.* If it does, organize a group of individuals to seek a meeting with the manager. As few as three people can be effective. Politely ask the manager to remove the materials. If he agrees, you've won. If he doesn't, move to *step two:* organizing.

As you begin to organize a picket, first find out if you'll need a permit. Many cities and counties require picketers to get a permit before they can legally organize in front of a pornography outlet. There will be a minimal fee for such a permit. To find out if you need one, contact your county clerk's office. The person there can then direct you to the appropriate city or county agency that issues the permits. Stay within the law!

Next you'll need to choose a picket chairman, media spokesperson, and a sign committee. The spokesperson is the only one authorized to speak for the group, since you want to speak with a single voice. Choose someone who is articulate, calm, and well-informed.

The third step involves the following elements: the availability of picketers, timing of the picket, and safety and preparation. Choose a time to picket when traffic outside the business is high. It takes a week to prepare signs, two weeks to acquire a picketing permit (if needed), and three weeks to promote the event properly.

As a picketer, you're exercising two rights guaranteed by the U.S. Constitution: freedom of speech and freedom of assembly. When picketing, keep in mind the following principles from the AFA:

♦ Picketers must remain on public property at all times.

♦ Never impede or block vehicle or pedestrian traffic. Do not harass any person entering the store nor try to talk to him.

♦ Only use signs that have been officially approved by your entire group. Keep them simple, direct, and polite. Avoid using defamatory slogans against the store owner.

♦ Refer the media to your appointed spokesperson.

♦ If you encounter counterpicketers, remain at peace with them unless you're threatened. You can call the police for protection.

♦ Conduct yourself in a Christlike manner.

You might also consider launching a Pornography Awareness Week or participating in a Victims of Pornography Month campaign. Find out more about Pornography Awareness Week through the AFA's Web site, www.afa.net. To be part of a Victims of Pornography Month, access the Victims of Pornography Web site for details: www.victimsofpornography.org. May has been designated as the annual Victims of Pornography month. This group provides media support for a nationwide campaign to draw attention to the serious damage porn causes in society. Its Web site is filled with testimonies, facts, and statistics.

Enough Is Enough! (EIE), founded by Dee Jepsen, has also published a helpful manual on how you can fight pornography in your community. The *What One*

Woman Can Do: Take Action Manual presents a detailed plan, including a 12-step program that every local group can adopt. Those steps are:

♦ Build a broad-based team

♦ Understand the harm, legal issues, and content of pornography

♦ Build a speakers bureau: your key to mobilizing a volunteer force

♦ Organize, manage, and maximize your volunteer force

♦ Raise funds

♦ Assist victims

♦ Build media relations

♦ Work within the law enforcement system

♦ Build public awareness

♦ Develop a legislative strategy

♦ Deal with video pornography

♦ Maintain the victories

EIE suggests that women concerned about pornography start a Cookie Patrol in front of pornography bookstores or video stores. These women will give each man entering the store a brochure on counseling for sexual addiction, plus a cookie. The cookies should be store-bought, not homemade, to avoid the possibility of legal liability should the cookies cause sickness.

The Cookie Patrol has three-woman teams working in rotating two-hour shifts while the facility is open. A Cookie Patrol is different in format and purpose from a picket; the women in a Cookie Patrol should feel free to speak to those entering the establishment if they wish to. (For safety purposes, though, several men should be waiting in cars nearby in case there's trouble.) Men entering these stores seem to be more embarrassed and convicted when women are handing out cookies and brochures than when men do it. For more details on EIE and the Cookie Patrol, access the EIE Web site: www.enough.org.

Take It to the Networks, Movie Studios, and Advertisers

As noted in earlier chapters, you don't have to watch television or movies for long to notice several common themes: extreme and gratuitous violence, explicit sex without consequences, homosexuality, and anti-Christian messages. MIM has published an important citizen's action guide to help concerned parents fight those things in the media. It contains a list of advertisers you can contact to protest their sponsorship of anti-social programming. The report, *Stranger in the House,* can be ordered from MIM at its Web site: www.morality inmedia.org.

Letter writing is one of the most effective and easiest ways to make an impact. As seen earlier in this chapter, you can complain to the FCC about raunchy programming, but you should also make your views known to advertisers (both national and local) who are sponsoring antisocial programs. You should complain, too, to local TV or radio stations, as well as the national networks, when you see or hear something that offends you. MIM's report on TV contains a list of addresses of advertisers and TV networks. The AFA has a similar report that lists advertisers and the shows they sponsor.

Never written such a letter before? Then consider these principles when contacting an advertiser:

♦ Don't begin with the assumption that the advertiser is actively supporting sexually explicit programming. Many times, ad agencies buy blocks of time for a company without the company's knowing which shows its commercials will air on.

♦ Begin your letter with praise and/or encouragement for its product if you've used it in the past.

♦ Express disappointment that the company's product is being associated with antisocial programming.

♦ Explain what you saw on the program, and ask if the sponsor is going to continue supporting this show.

♦ Provide facts to back up your concerns about the harmful effects of sexual, violent, or antireligious messages.

♦ Make specific requests (e.g., to stop advertising on the program in question), and ask for a specific response.

♦ If you get a negative response, write a second letter, letting the company know you're going to boycott its product and tell others about its refusal to stop supporting antisocial programs. Then stick with your boycott!

If you're writing to networks, use the same general plan. If they refuse to change, let them know you're going to stop watching their channels altogether until they begin sponsoring prosocial programs. You can also let the advertisers know you're boycotting the networks. Please keep in mind, however, that you're not personally responsible for fighting every TV show that offends you. Pick a few worthy targets, then keep after them until you see results. Pray for others to get involved as well so you can multiply your efforts.

MAKING A DIFFERENCE

You can make a difference in your community! Don't make the mistake, though, of thinking the pornography plague in your town is all on your shoulders. You'll need help. With the aid of just a few people who share your concern for the people of your town—especially the children—you can make a huge impact.

Remember, though, that it takes time, determination, and prayer to bring about lasting social change. Once you start, keep at it. This is not a sprint; it's a marathon. The problem has been developing for a long time, and it will take a long time to turn things around. Also, remember that you're not going to win without hardship. This struggle isn't for cowards. The Bible says, "Let us not become weary in doing good, for at the proper time we will reap a harvest if we do not give up" (Galatians 6:9). We should all tape that verse on our refrigerators or computers as a constant reminder of God's promise. The outcome is in His hands ultimately, but He uses people like us to carry out His will. Are we ready?

CHAPTER EIGHT

What If Your Child Has Been Exposed to Pornography?

Genna was introduced to pornography at the age of 11 when her grandmother gave her some romance novels. Although she came from a good Christian home, Genna began obsessing on these books and spent hours fantasizing about men. When she was only 12, her parents allowed her to date a 15-year-old boy. This young man was involved in pornography and began "mentoring" Genna in sexual experimentation. Their relationship eventually led to frequent oral and phone sex.

Unaware of what was happening, Genna slowly developed a serious sexual addiction. It worsened as a result of her baby-sitting for various members of her church; in a number of their homes, she discovered pornographic magazines and sex manuals.

On the outside, Genna seemed like the perfect Christian girl. She was successful in high school and became a popular student at her Christian college. Although she remained a physical virgin until marriage, she obsessively engaged in oral sex and other sexual activities with boys.

Like many sex addicts, Genna successfully led a double life for years. She remained physically faithful to her husband, but she indulged in a pornographic fantasy life. Her secret was finally exposed when her husband discovered a torrid romance novel in their living room. He later found her at the family computer at 4:00 in the morning, accessing pornography Web sites.

Genna and her husband have been in therapy on and off for nearly 15 years at the time of this writing, working through her addiction. Both are committed Christians who are truly seeking God's healing power in their lives.

We tell this story for three reasons: First, we want to reiterate that boys are not the only ones vulnerable to pornography. In the past, girls seldom got involved in viewing hard-core materials (although this is rapidly changing because of the Internet). Now, girls and women become hooked on pornography mostly through the "gateway" of romance novels and Internet chat rooms or forums.

Second, because Genna had made a commitment to Jesus Christ, attended church, and said and done all the right things outwardly, she seemed to be the model Christian girl. Regrettably, we can be fooled by appearances.

Third, it is possible that, like Genna, your child may be hiding a secret addiction.

NORMAL CURIOSITY?

It's normal for children to be curious about sexual matters—especially when puberty hits. And, despite our best efforts to the contrary, they will invariably be exposed to pornography at some point. So how tolerant should a parent be of a child's exposure to sexual images in magazines, on TV, on the Internet, or in movies or videos? While a parent should not overreact to a child's exposure to porn or immediately assume he is destined to become a sexual predator, there's really no need to be "tolerant" of his exposure to sexual images.

As we've seen earlier in this book, choosing to use pornography is clearly contrary to God's Word and will—a sin—because porn's only purpose is to incite lust. Further, we've seen the many ways in which porn harms and eventually enslaves its users, hurting not only them but also those they love (as when a man is bound to the Centerfold Syndrome and unable to relate to his wife in a healthy way) and those they may victimize.

Thus, we urge you not to adopt the casual attitude that "boys will be boys," that using pornography is just another, normal part of growing up. If you learn that your child has been viewing porn in any form, it's not a time to panic, but it is cause for serious alarm. You need to be ready to take action to mitigate its effects, and also to cut off future access.

WARNING SIGNS OF A POSSIBLE PORN ADDICTION

If you haven't actually discovered any pornography use by your child, what are some telltale signs that there might be a problem? (Remember that kids become experts at hiding illicit behaviors.) According to Rob Jackson in an interview with the authors, here are several possible indicators:

♦ **Distractibility.** Your child may display emotional characteristics akin to Attention Deficit Disorder (ADD) or Attention Deficit Hyperactivity Disorder (ADHD). He may be unable to concentrate while studying or talking to you. He may be fidgety.

♦ **A "Drunken" Humor About Sex.** He may constantly discuss sexual matters in a humorous way. His eyes may get wide; his countenance may change; he may display muscle tension and rapid breathing as he jokes about sex.

♦ **Moodiness.** Most adolescents are already moody because of the physical and emotional changes they're experiencing. But a sexually addicted child may display anger or anxiety if you deprive him of TV, video, or Internet privileges. The addict wants his "fix" regularly.

Accessing porn, to a sex addict, is like a drug addict shooting up with heroin or snorting cocaine. When denied his fix, he becomes angry, depressed, and hostile.

◆ **Unaccounted-for Periods of Time.** You may discover that your child said he was going to the mall or a movie, but he actually went somewhere else. He may also spend an inordinate amount of time on the Internet. In addition, he may begin spending hours at the public or school library. If such visits are out of character for him, he may not be studying but accessing pornography on unfiltered computers.

◆ **Deceit and Theft.** Your child may start lying to you about what he and his friends are doing after school. You may begin finding money missing from your wallet or purse, as a child addicted to porn will often steal from his parents to purchase more. Or he may start shoplifting. (I [Frank] did both these things when I was 11 and 12 years old. I took money from my mom's purse to buy comic books, but I also shoplifted two or three girlie magazines and slipped them inside the comics. If the Internet had existed back in the mid 1950s, I would have quickly become a full-blown porn addict.)

◆ **Sexually Stimulating Materials in His Room.** Your child may have sexually provocative wall posters, music, or magazines in his room.

◆ **Sexually Stimulating Clothing Styles.** Watch for the kinds of clothing tastes your child is developing. Is your daughter wearing tight, revealing clothes? Is your son wearing attire that models the rap culture or T-shirts with sexual innuendos on them?

Of course, if your child is already exhibiting obviously out-of-control sexual behavior or isn't even trying to hide a sexual obsession, you missed the early warning signs and have a serious problem on your hands.

LOOKING FOR ANSWERS

We realize that the warning signals in the preceding section might also be signs of drug abuse or just general rebellion. That's why, if you observe them, you'll want to investigate what's going on. *Please do not assume that your child is immune to a sexual addiction—especially if you have not yet taken steps to prevent him from being exposed to pornographic materials.* What may be only a small concern now could grow into major trouble if it isn't dealt with. As we've seen in earlier chapters, and as Genna's story at the beginning of this chapter illustrates, Christians struggle in this area just like everyone else.

Further Indicators

Bill Perkins, in *When Good Men Are Tempted*, credits therapist Patrick Carnes for identifying four clear indicators that a person has become addicted to compulsive sexual behaviors: (1) The sexual behavior is done in secret, and the person frequently lies to cover up his actions. (2) The behavior can become abusive and exploitative of others. (3) The behavior is used to deaden painful feelings. (4) The behavior is empty of genuine commitment and caring.

On Rob Jackson's Web site, www.sexualintegrity.org, he offers this warning to parents:

> Perhaps your child … has already begun to show signs of vulnerability in this area. Before the age of Internet, the median [most frequent] age of exposure to pornography was 11 to 13 years of age. Frankly, I believe today's children are at a greater risk of earlier exposure. We can only expect that earlier exposure to a greater variety and severity of pornography will produce a more treatment-resistant sex addict.… [But] through God's design, children are more resilient than we realize, and change can occur when we intervene sooner rather than later.

Thus, if your child shows some of the warning signs described above or you have other reason to suspect pornography use and/or sexual addiction, you should strongly consider conducting a thorough search of his room, including videos, CDs, computer hard drive, floppy disks, magazines, and clothing.

"But is that really okay?" you might ask. "Isn't that an invasion of my child's privacy?" Since a good parent-child relationship is based on mutual respect, those are good questions to ask. However, if you have reason to be concerned, you have the right and indeed the *responsibility* to find out if your child is involved in any kind of behavior that may be destructive to him and your family. Besides, your child's room belongs to you! It's your home, and you're entitled to take action to keep it safe.

If you strongly suspect that your child is involved in pornography, Jackson also suggests that you read his diary. Jackson notes that in many of his counseling cases involving sexual abuse or promiscuity, the only way parents learned of their child's problem was by reading his or her diary. The knowledge those parents gained was instrumental in getting their children the help they needed.

This may strike some parents as especially invasive and a violation of a child's right to privacy, but what's the alternative? Good parenting means keeping close watch on your child—and that means reading his diary if necessary to protect him.

If you have cause for concern about your child (such as the presence of some of the warning signs of sexual addiction), Jackson further recommends taking a hard look at any sexually stimulating material in your child's room. Seductive posters, photos, CD jackets and lyrics, videos, and the like can cause him to fantasize about sex. And fantasy, notes Jackson, is one of the three major building blocks of a sexual addiction. (The other two are feeding on pornographic materials and masturbation.) So if there's anything in your child's room that might cause him to think impure thoughts, you have the right to remove it.

If you feel compelled to take such action, however, take the time to explain yourself—to remind your child of the importance of remaining sexually pure and of the ways in which porn in any form works to destroy purity.

REPAIRING THE DAMAGE

In the event that you discover your child has, indeed, been viewing pornography, how should you respond? We posed this question in an interview with Dr. Mark Laaser, a former partner with Rob Jackson in the Christian Alliance for Sexual Recovery and now head of Faithful & True Ministries, a nationwide outreach to sex addicts. Laaser became hooked on pornography at age 11 and had a 25-year struggle to overcome a major sexual addiction that included prostitutes and adultery. Thus, he counsels from painful personal experience as well as professional expertise.

Laaser suggests you take the following steps if you discover your child is accessing pornography:

◆ First, before you discuss your discovery with your child, make sure you and your spouse are in agreement about what to say. If you're not, you're only going to muddy the moral waters when you bring up the topic. Your child needs to see that you're united and acting as one. If you feel you need counsel from your pastor, Christian counselor, or even police department, please get it. And pray about your response before moving ahead, asking God for His wisdom, insight, and heart on this.

◆ When you talk to your child about your discovery, avoid shaming him. Instead of first asking him where he got the material, ask, "How did you feel when you looked at it?" and give him an opportunity to explain. Then tell him that while it's normal for a child to be curious about sexual matters, it's important that he learn about sex and sexuality from his parents, not from his peers, magazines, movies, or the Internet.

♦ Point out that it's also normal for him to be tempted to view things he shouldn't. Either you or your spouse can relate how you may have been sexually tempted in the past. Emphasize that your child is not weird or perverted.

♦ Offer your love and fellowship. Let him know you're going to help him work through this problem, praying for him daily (if you haven't already been doing so) and holding him accountable for his behavior in this area. Explain again the dangers inherent in accessing this material. You can liken porn to crack cocaine in its addictive powers. (Use information from chapter 1 on the impact that sexual images have on the brain.) Point out that viewing these images can eventually lead to damaged relationships and sinful actions if not stopped.

♦ Explain what restrictions you will now impose to help him avoid any future involvement with pornographic materials. If you haven't already done so, remove his computer (especially if it has had unlimited Web access) and TV from his room. Subscribe to an Internet filtering system. Remove any sexually stimulating materials from his room. Control his relationships with others who may be supplying him with porn.

Now let's expand on those steps a little. As you talk with your child, let him know that you consider this situation, like all times of struggle, to be a wonderful opportunity for you to draw closer to each other and to God. Perhaps you as a parent have been spending too much time in work or in ministry to others, neglecting your own family's needs. It may be that God wants to teach you more about prayer, persistence, and forgiveness.

Remind your child how much God loves him. He wants the best for him, and He has given him parents to help protect him from the dangerous influences in our culture. Emphasize, too, the reality of Satan as one who seeks to rob and destroy God's people.

As a parent, you also need to admit if you've contributed to the problem by maintaining a collection of porn or keeping other magazines that teeter on the edge of being pornographic. Do you read *Cosmopolitan* or tabloids with explicit photos in them? Car magazines frequently contain seductive shots of scantily clad women. Bodybuilding magazines also feature nearly nude women. Do you leave Victoria's Secret catalogs lying around the house? Do you read steamy romance novels? Do you watch TV shows or movies on cable or video that are sexually provocative? Do you visit Web sites or chat rooms that are even mildly sexually oriented?

As we've suggested before, you may have to make some tough decisions about your child's friends. If they're contributing in some way to his inclination toward sexual sin, you may have to limit the time and places that he can be with them. Again, explain to your

child that you're doing this because it's your responsibility to protect him.

As you discuss these things with your child, you can
compare pornography's appeal to a virus that invades a
person's body to make him ill or even kill him. Pornography is a moral virus that must be fought with the
power of prayer, reasonable precautions, and accountability.

ENCOURAGING POSITIVE GROWTH

Besides doing all you can to keep pornography away
from your child, while holding him accountable for his
actions, it's also helpful to encourage positive spiritual
growth. A person who has gotten hooked on porn has
directed a lot of energy toward his habit. You can help
redirect that energy by getting him involved in more
activities at church or school. Physical exercise can dis-
sipate much of that energy as well.

Another good idea is to do an age-appropriate Bible
study with your child on God's view of sex and marriage. His thought life needs to be cleansed of bad
images and replaced with positive images of healthy
sexuality. Focus on the Family has produced two excellent resources that you can use in conjunction with this
effort. *In Your Face ... In Your Mind* and *Fantasy World:
Pure Thinking in a Sea of Unrealistic Images* are written
for teenagers but can be used with younger children,

too. *In Your Face* is for boys, and *Fantasy World* is for girls.

Steve Watters, author of *In Your Face*, makes the case that while God created sex for our enjoyment within marriage, the use of pornography can damage our sexuality, our minds, and our emotions. Watters observes that a boy who has been exposed to pornography must recommit himself to following God's plan for sexuality. The process comprises three elements: confession, accountability, and mental transformation.

Brad, a former porn addict, described his transformation process in *In Your Face*: "I began to invest in relationships, get into God's Word, seek Him in prayer and step out of the mold that pornography had cast me in. Sometimes I didn't want to put forth the effort, but to come to a complete healing, it was something I had to do. So I began to reach out to others, read more, pray more and talk more. My emphasis shifted from myself to the people around me, and I began to care again. I noticed that I was much less susceptible to lust when I was actively pursuing relationships with others. It was a hard road to travel, but the alternative was literally destroying me, and I was determined that I was going to make it."

As you can see, it isn't enough just to cut off access to pornography. Something must fill the void left in your child's heart. Fill it with God's Word, wholesome activities, accountability, fervent prayer, and godly friendships.

Stained-Glass Windows: Helping Kids Put the Pieces Together

Author, camp director, and dad Joe White offers the following advice for helping a child better understand how God can make something good come out of our bad experiences:

The fine art of making Romans 8:28 a reality in the life of your [child] is a huge challenge—but a wonderful one. Every young person will go through pain and brokenness, especially in today's tragic world. Every young person needs to know that all those things *do* work together for good when God gets His hands on them.

How can you turn your [child's] traumas into opportunities for spiritual growth? I've found it helpful to use a word picture with my kids, that of stained-glass windows.

As I've told my children, God is in the business of building stained-glass windows. None of His "paintings" are on canvas. They're all made of thousands of broken pieces, skillfully picked up and dusted off and soldered together into magnificent murals. The broken pieces are made of our hurts and hard times. With my kids I've used examples of my own hurts, and theirs, to show how God is slowly making stained-glass windows of our lives.

Employing this word picture with your [child] is not an overnight experience. It takes lots of asking the "What's wrong?" and "How do you feel?" and "What are you doing about it?" questions, not to mention hours of warmth and empathy and unconditional regard. You need to build up a bank account of together time and tender moments in order to make the word picture meaningful.

Once you've done that, and once the moment comes when your child's heart breaks ..., you can use the word picture. You can sit down with your [child] and say, "God makes stained-glass windows. Let's look at yours."[1]

YOUR LAST RESORT: GETTING PROFESSIONAL HELP

So far in this chapter, we've described things that you can do as a parent to help a child who has been exposed to pornography. But some children need more assistance than parents can provide. They need the care of an experienced, Christian professional.

To determine if your child needs such help, you'll have to make a sober judgment about just how far along he or she may be on the road to a sexual addiction. Begin by asking your child the following questions, and then refer back to the section in this chapter on the warning signs of a sexual addict:

◆ What kinds of materials have you been looking at? (He may be viewing rape, bestiality, homosexual conduct, or sadomasochism. Each of these will require a slightly different therapeutic approach if counseling is needed.)

◆ How long have you been viewing this material?

◆ Where did you first get access to it? Are your friends involved?

◆ Do you look at this material every day?

◆ Are you trying to find more of this material? Have you stolen pornographic magazines or videos?

◆ What do you feel like when you can't look at this material? Do you become nervous, frustrated, or angry?

◆ Do you think about this all day long?

◆ Have you acted out any of the things you've seen?

◆ Do you feel as if you've lost control over this in your life?

Your next steps will depend on the honesty of the answers you receive to those questions. If your child has only recently been exposed to a pornography magazine or Internet site and hasn't progressed any further, you can take the commonsense measures we've suggested to cut off any further access and encourage positive growth. *With prayer and open discussion with your child, the damage should be minimal.*

If, however, your child indicates that his porn use has become routine and has been happening for a long time (a month or more), and he's showing clear signs of compulsive, obsessive behavior (or movement in that direction), you would be wise to seek professional help. As you consider this option, keep these facts in mind:

First, you're going to need a Christian counselor, although you may be hard-pressed to find one in your area with the expertise you need. In the back of this book, we'll list resources for finding a good counselor.

Second, if your child is not a threat to himself or others, insurance may not pay for therapy. This means you'll have to carry the entire expense, a fact that deters many from getting the help they need.

Third, you may opt for a secular 12-step program like Sexaholics Anonymous, or you may find help through such Christian organizations as Faithful & True, which has established accountability support groups in various churches throughout the U.S.

Faithful & True groups are based on the following principles:

• *Humility.* The sexual acting out in our lives and

the consequences of this self-medicating lifestyle remind us of how useless those behaviors have been in controlling our lives.

♦ *Surrender*. Only a relationship with Jesus Christ can provide true healing as we are willing to completely submit to God's will for our lives.

♦ *Confession*. We have found that only in being honest with our Savior and other healthy Christians can we be healed from the shame of our lives.

♦ *Sanctification*. We constantly seek to be more Christlike in our character.

♦ *Forgiveness and restoration*. By admitting our mistakes to others, taking responsibility for our actions, and seeking to right the wrongs of the past, we can find forgiveness in Christ.

♦ *Spiritual discipline*. We remain accountable for our current behaviors and daily seek to improve our intimate relationship with Jesus Christ.

♦ *Evangelism*. Remembering our previous loneliness and despair, and being responsible for the progress in our own recovery, we seek to share that hope and healing with others.[2]

Fourth, you may need to get your child into a rehabilitation program if he is seriously addicted and/or resistant to help. Locate a Christian or state-run program that provides intensive and personalized care in a structured environment. If your child has not yet moved beyond viewing pornography to acting out his sexual addiction, one of these may be a good solution. (We'll list some rehabilitation facilities at the end of this book.)

By "acting out," we mean the child is molesting another child, becoming a Peeping Tom, or exposing himself in public. These are crimes and, obviously, indicators of a serious problem. It's understandable that you would want to protect your reputation and your child from the consequences of his actions, but your greater concern should be that he be prevented from injuring others.

What to Expect

If you conclude that your child needs to see a professional counselor, what can you expect to have happen after you've made that terrifying phone call? Rob Jackson's treatment process is typical:

First, he invites the parents in for an initial consultation. He needs to learn from them if both husband and wife are in agreement about their child's problem and the course of treatment. If they're not, he is unlikely to be able to make progress.

He lets them know that his job is to provide counsel in a safe and professional environment. That means he will not touch the client at any time; there will be no hugging or other expressions of consolation in order to avoid any appearance of impropriety. In addition, he will never deride the experience of the child or engage in humor. There will be no shaming during therapy, either.

Jackson then explains his profession's and the state's requirements about confidentiality. He tells them when he is legally obligated to break a confidence. One of the most obvious examples is when there has been sexual molestation.

He also explains to the parents about each individual's right to privacy during the sessions. Both parents and children have a certain right to privacy. The therapist has the discretion to keep things from the parents if revealing them would further damage the child. If the child, however, reveals something the parents should know, he will encourage the child to tell them. Parents, of course, are entitled to know anything that puts their child at risk.

After going through these explanations, Jackson usually describes his own faith in Jesus Christ and how it will be integrated into the treatment of their child.

At some point during this meeting or in a subsequent appointment, Jackson will go over the pornographic materials the child had been viewing, which the parents will have brought in a sealed bag. After making notes on the contents, Jackson will destroy the materials on the spot by shredding or some other means. The materials will not be tossed in a wastebasket, where others may find them, nor will they be stored away, because *he* might then be tempted to view them. As Jackson says, pornography has the power to contaminate whoever it touches.

When Jackson has a good idea of where the parents are coming from after one or two initial consultations, he will make an appointment for them to bring in their child. The first of those sessions—or all of them—are open to both parents and child if that is their wish.

As Jackson first encounters the youngster, he begins by asking him to explain if he knows why he is there. This usually frees the child to unload a great deal of guilt, shame, and pent-up feelings about his struggles. This is typically a listening interview, with Jackson taking notes. By the next session, he will have processed his notes and his observations and will be ready with a series of questions for the child.

Jackson compares his work with the child to dealing with an iceberg. The tip of the iceberg is the sexual addiction, but the therapist's goal is to go down through it to find the root causes of the child's initial need to access pornographic materials.

In the beginning of this investigative process, Jackson will explain to the child what he has done wrong and that these wrongs can be remedied. He will then move on to a more intellectual discussion of sex and the sanctity of marriage, the impact of pornographic images on the brain, and so on. Next he will try to give the child a clear understanding of God's plan for sex and how pornography distorts this. He then explores the emotional aspects of the child's sexual addiction to discover the traumas that may have caused him to be vulnerable to porn. As Jackson notes, however, with the advent of the Internet, children who have experienced no trauma in their lives are becoming quickly and seriously addicted without passing through soft-core porn to hard-core materials. All of it is instantly available and devastating to a child's moral development.

After working through the emotional issues, Jackson then deals with the child's spiritual life—his walk with Christ, his understanding of sin and salvation, and his views of Jesus Christ, the Holy Spirit, and holiness.

The goal, of course, is to see emotional and spiritual transformation in the child's life and a deliverance from the addiction. There's no quick fix for a sexual addiction, however. The process may be long and painful—but it must be pursued.

Jackson says that when a couple comes to him with their addicted child, they are totally bankrupt of hope. But their mutual faith in Jesus Christ can give them the hope they need to endure and grow from this experience, no matter how horrifying it may be.

IS THERE HOPE?

Dr. Mark Laaser believes there is hope for every person who has become addicted to pornography. That hope comes first from the opportunity to experience the power of God at work in your life. A person may experience total healing through that power, once and for all, or he may rely on God's power each day to keep him pure. Laaser observes, "Those of us who have worked through an addiction know what our hope really is: to come to a more intimate relationship with Jesus Christ. In any kind of sexual struggle, you find out how truly powerless you really are."

Laaser believes that the struggling addict—no matter what he's addicted to—can actually live a more fulfilling life than someone who has never experienced such a struggle. Why? Because the addict has had to come face-to-face with the fact that he's utterly power-less to change his behavior without total dependence on God. As Laaser says, the realization of your total power-lessness is a "good thing and a tremendous opportunity for tremendous things to happen."

Second, hope comes in the realization that though our spiritual journey is opposed by Satan—who prowls around like a lion, seeking whom he may devour—and by a sex-saturated culture that constantly seeks to per-vert the things of God, our minds can be transformed and renewed in harmony with that of Jesus Christ. The familiar words of Romans 12:2 tell us: "Do not conform any longer to the pattern of this world, but be trans-formed by the renewing of your mind. Then you will be able to test and approve what God's will is—his good, pleasing and perfect will."

As we parents continually work with our children to see that their minds are transformed and that they do not conform to the world's standards and practices, we can deal with problems of pride and individual sin in our own lives and in the lives of our children. In addi-tion, when a child has the courage to admit to his most embarrassing sins, the experience teaches him how to be genuine and intimate with others. "You're teaching a child to say the worst things he's ever done, and when he finds out that he can still be accepted and loved, that's a huge lesson for him to learn. This process sets him up to be open to intimacy for the rest of his life," says Laaser. (To help foster your child's spiritual growth, we again recommend Focus on the Family's *Parents' Guide to the Spiritual Growth of Children* and *Parents' Guide to the Spiritual Mentoring of Teens*.)

In every Faithful & True support group, they begin each session with the Serenity Prayer, which you may also wish to pray for yourself and your child:

> *God, grant me the serenity to accept the things I cannot*
> *change,*
> *The courage to change the things I can,*
> *And the wisdom to know the difference.*
> *Living one day at a time, enjoying one moment at a time;*
> *Accepting hardships as a pathway to peace;*
> *Taking, as Jesus did, this sinful world as it is, not as I*
> *would have it;*
> *Trusting that You will make all things right if I surrender to*
> *Your will;*
> *So that I may be reasonably happy in this life*
> *And supremely happy with You forever in the next. Amen.*

CHAPTER NINE

Conclusion: Never Forget That This Is a Spiritual War

As we were finishing this last chapter, several pornography-related stories hit the news. Each of them added to our sense of urgency to complete this book.

♦ In Nashville, Tennessee, a 13-year-old boy was arrested on rape charges after allegedly sexually assaulting a six-year-old boy and a seven-year-old girl. The boy said he got his sexual ideas from viewing pornography sites on the Internet. His mother and father were separated. The mother had a filtering system on her computer; the father did not. When the boy visited his father's home, he frequently accessed porn. This youngster had no prior criminal record, but now he's an accused rapist, and his alleged victims will need ongoing counseling to work through the trauma of being sexually assaulted.

♦ In Virginia, a federal-court judge threw out the state's "harmful to minors" law dealing with Internet pornography. The lawsuit was brought by a homosexual Web site and People for the American Way (PAW), founded by TV producer Norman Lear. At the time of this writing, similar laws have been struck down in New Mexico, Wisconsin, and Michigan, while laws protecting minors from Internet porn have been upheld in California.

♦ PAW threatened to sue the Nashua, New Hampshire, library system for putting filtering systems on all its computers. Fearful of being bankrupted in a costly lawsuit, the library system pulled filters from its main computers, but it left them on the children's computers.

♦ During the summer of 2000, the Internet newspaper *WorldNetDaily* published an exposé on Clinton White House personnel accessing vast quantities of pornography videos from teen, homosexual, and bestiality Web sites. This story was not widely reported in the mainstream media, but it clearly demonstrated why the Clinton Administration was so lax in enforcing our nation's anti-obscenity laws. According to a computer expert brought into the White House to beef up Internet security, the majority of the Internet traffic coming into the White House was pornography. High-level officials were involved.

Unfortunately, this list could go on for pages. There is an exponential growth of pornography on the Internet and elsewhere, and groups like the American Civil Liberties Union, PAW, and the American Library Association are determined to keep our society wide open to the porn industry.

This is deadly serious business. Your child could become a sex crime perpetrator or a victim of pornography. Or he may develop warped ideas about sexuality by viewing a wide range of deviant sex sites on the Web. At the very least, every child who succumbs to the lure of porn will develop (to one degree or another) a case of Centerfold Syndrome, which will make it difficult if not impossible for him to have healthy, God- and spouse-honoring relationships in the future.

Contrary to what the "anything goes" groups believe, children have no right to unrestricted access to pornographic materials.

PROTECTING YOUR CHILD IS A SPIRITUAL BATTLE!

As we've seen in this book, porn has seeped into just about every corner of our society. Even places that, in the past, parents could reasonably assume were safe havens for children—like the local library or the public school classroom—now can hold great moral danger.

As we've also seen, however, parents can take positive action to keep pornography out of their home and to prepare their children for exposure to it from other sources. Moms and dads can also oppose the purveyors of porn in their community, making it a safer environment for everyone's kids. And if and when their children are exposed to pornography, parents can help to mitigate its effects and bring healing.

In the midst of doing all that, though, we must

One Man's Victory

Christian vocalist Clay Crosse struggled with pornography for many years. He was first introduced to porn at a friend's house when he was 10 years old. Crosse recalls seeing pornography several times during the next few years: "Even though it wasn't many times, the small amount of exposure was enough to leave lasting images that ultimately became damaging."

When Crosse got married, pornography was not a part of his life, but he had lustful thoughts that affected his view of women in general and his wife in particular. He was allowing sexual messages to affect him through the TV, movies, magazine articles, music, and comedians. "Pretty soon my thought life was wandering. I began to remember those images of porn that I'd seen over the years and desired to see them again."

In 1998, after eight years of marriage, Crosse realized he had a serious problem. As he flew home from a concert in Seattle, he became convicted about his lustful attitudes. "I realized I was at my lowest point. I saw myself for what I was—a man crumbling in the hold of lust."

Crosse eventually confessed his lustful thoughts to his wife and repented. He hopes to help other men avoid falling into sexual temptations.

never lose sight of the fact that at its core, the struggle to protect our children in an X-rated world is a spiritual battle. Our ultimate enemy is not the pornographers but the forces of darkness that animate them. And our ultimate victory will come not from our own efforts but from the guidance, strength, healing, and heart-changing power of our Lord.

Thus, protecting our kids calls for both prayer and action! The Bible tells us in Ephesians 6:10-18 that we must put on the full armor of God in order to defend ourselves from the devil's schemes. The apostle Paul wrote, "For our struggle is not against flesh and blood, but against the rulers, against the authorities, against the powers of this dark world and against the spiritual forces of evil in the heavenly realms."

Paul then explained that we are put on the belt of truth, the breastplate of righteousness, the shield of faith ("with which you can extinguish all the flaming arrows of the evil one"), the helmet of salvation, and the sword of the Spirit (God's Word). Paul also urged us to "pray in the Spirit on all occasions with all kinds of prayers and requests."

Make it a top priority to pray *every day* that your child will be protected from exposure to pornography and inappropriate sexual messages at school and else-where. Pray that God will give you wisdom and revela-tion to know if your child is hiding something from you. And, most important of all, make sure your child has a saving faith in Jesus Christ. Being a Christian won't automatically deliver your child from a potential pornography addiction, but it will give him the spiritual resources to resist temptation and to deal honestly with you if he's struggling.

Pray not only for your child and yourself, but also for your family, friends, neighbors, church family, and community. Pornography addiction is a silent epidemic, both inside and outside the church. Pray that God will turn hearts and minds to a biblical standard of right and wrong, moral and immoral, safe and unsafe, especially in this area of human sexuality that He meant for great good between husband and wife but that our culture has greatly corrupted.

Protecting your child in an X-rated world can seem, at times, an overwhelming task. But with God on your side, you *can* succeed. May He richly bless you and your family in that vital effort.

Pornography
and the Law

❧

In September 2000, in Canton, Ohio, a six-year-old boy was suspended from school after students on a bus saw him standing naked through a window of his home. According to the boy's mother, he had a doctor's appointment and was disappointed to miss his class's field trip. Mom placed him in the bathtub so that he wouldn't see the bus arrive at its usual time. The boy's sister, however, knocked on the bathroom door to alert him that the bus had arrived, and the little cherub ran from the bathtub to the window and shouted for the driver to wait.

The principal learned of the incident at school and met with the superintendent to discuss the matter. Because the boy had been nude, they decided to file charges against him as they considered such behavior to be sexual harassment of the children aboard the bus. According to the boy's attorney, school officials withdrew the charges and suspension, but not before they made the six-year-old sign a document acknowledging that he understood the charges. The attorney said that the boy had just learned to write; when he signed his name, it was trailing off at the end. The family is seeking $5,000 in cash to set up a college fund for the boy.

How have we come to a time when public schools have zero tolerance for "sexual harassment" by innocent six-year-olds? It is due in large measure to a sex-obsessed culture, to advertising and entertainment industries that target, exploit, and victimize children with sexual images.

Also in September 2000, some not-so-innocent kindergarten children in a New York public school were suspended for engaging in sex acts on campus. When young children are caught engaging in sexual conduct and are asked where they learned such behavior, they commonly admit to having seen pornography.

What these incidents illustrate is yet more of the creeping overflow of our modern culture of pornography. As you seek to protect your child from the great harm that can come from exposure to porn, it's helpful to know what the law says about the subject. Whether your immediate concern is the offerings on your cable TV system, the Internet, or what youngsters might see at your local bookstore, there are federal, state, and local laws governing what is and isn't permissible. Being more familiar with the principles that underlie them can help you determine your best course of action as a concerned parent.

The inescapable fact is that much that you and we would consider pornographic is nonetheless legal and protected by the Supreme Court's current interpretation of the First Amendment. We'll look at the basic distinctions between what is and isn't legal, and then we'll describe in more detail those kinds of material that fall clearly outside the cover of law.

LEGAL PORNOGRAPHY

Pornography is a generic term that includes both legal and illegal materials. Pornography is generally defined as "all sexually oriented material intended primarily to arouse the reader, viewer, or listener."[1]

Legal pornography includes serious works of art, literature, politics, or science; mere nudity; medical works; and so on.[2] Soft-core pornography represents only a fraction of the material on the market today. The reason is simple—it doesn't titillate because porn users quickly become desensitized and need more-graphic material in order to be aroused and gratified.

ILLEGAL PORNOGRAPHY

Pornography that is not protected by the First Amendment is illegal. It includes obscenity ("hard-core," with penetration clearly visible); child pornography (depiction of a child engaged in sexual conduct by himself or with another); material harmful to minors displayed or distributed to minors (soft-core pornography); broadcast indecency (transmitted during a prohibited time period); and indecent dial-a-porn (transmitted without a written request by an adult).

Criminalizing the publication and distribution of materials that are not protected by the First Amendment is not censorship; it is not a prior restraint by the government of speech or expressive conduct. In *Alexander v. United States*, the Supreme Court addressed the issue of prior restraint and held: "Finally petitioner's proposed definition of the term 'prior restraint' would undermine the time-honored distinction between barring speech in the future and penalizing past speech.... Our decisions have steadfastly preserved the distinctions between prior restraints and subsequent punishments."[3]

Obscenity

Obscenity is not and never has been protected by the First Amendment. It is illegal to display or distribute to any person regardless of age or consent.

> Implicit in the history of the First Amendment is
> the rejection of obscenity as utterly without
> redeeming social importance. This rejection for
> that reason is mirrored in the universal judgment
> that obscenity should be restrained, reflected in the
> international agreement of over 50 nations, in the

obscenity laws of all 48 states, and in the 20
obscenity laws enacted by the Congress from 1842
to 1956. We hold that obscenity is not within the
area of constitutionally protected speech or press.[4]

Those are the words of one of the most ardent sup-
porters of the First Amendment, U.S. Supreme Court
Justice William Brennan, who wrote the Court's plural-
ity opinion in *Roth v. United States* in 1957.

"I know it when I see it." Ask most people what
obscenity is and they will repeat Supreme Court Justice
Potter Stewart's famous comment. Pornographers and
their allies love to quote Stewart in an attempt to con-
vince the rest of us that it's impossible to know what
obscenity is. They never quote all he said, however.
Stewart wrote that "under the First and Fourteenth
Amendments criminal laws in this area are constitutionally limited to hard-core pornography.... I shall not
today attempt further to define the kinds of material I
understand to be embraced within that shorthand
description; and perhaps I could never succeed in intel-
ligibly doing so. But I know it when I see it".[5] Stewart
said that obscenity is "hard-core pornography."

Pornographers also fail to quote Stewart two years
later in *Ginzburg v. United States*[6] when he clearly
described the kind of hard-core pornography that may
be found obscene. Stewart wrote:

There does exist a distinct and easily identifiable
class of material in which all of these elements

coalesce. It is that, and that alone, which I think government may constitutionally suppress, whether by
criminal or civil sanctions. I have referred to such
material before as hardcore pornography, without trying further to define it.... In order to prevent any possible misunderstanding, I have set out in the margin
a description, borrowed from the Solicitor General's
brief, of the kind of thing to which I have refer-
ence.... Such materials include photographs, both
still and motion picture, with no pretense of artistic
value, graphically depicting acts of sexual intercourse, including various acts of sodomy and sadism,
and sometimes involving several participants in
scenes of orgy-like character. They also include strips
of drawings in comic-book format grossly depicting
similar activities in an exaggerated fashion. There
are, in addition, pamphlets and booklets, sometimes
with photographic illustrations, verbally describing
such activities in a bizarre manner with no attempt
whatsoever to afford portrayals of character or situation and with no pretense to literary value. All of this
material ... cannot conceivably be characterized as
embodying communication of ideas or artistic values
inviolate under the First Amendment.

In 1973, for the first time, a majority of the Supreme
Court agreed on a definition of obscenity in *Miller v.
California.*[7] The *Miller* definition has been used by federal and state juries in hundreds of obscenity cases to
find hard-core pornography obscene. It remains the test

for obscenity in every medium, including print, television, radio, recordings, dial-a-porn, movies, videos, E-mail, telephone, and interactive computer services.

The federal law prohibits the sale of, or possession with intent to sell, obscene material on federal land,[8] by U.S. mail,[9] using a common carrier, including an interactive computer service through interstate and foreign commerce,[10] radio broadcasting,[11] transportation or travel in interstate or foreign commerce or an interactive computer service for purpose of sale or distribution,[12] engaging in the business of selling or transferring or receiving obscene material that has been shipped in interstate or foreign commerce, including interactive computer services,[13] through cable or subscription television,[14] and using the mail or interstate or foreign commerce to knowingly transfer obscene matter to a minor.[15] The federal law also provides for forfeiture of any and all assets connected to dissemination of obscene material.[16]

It is not illegal to possess obscene material (except child pornography, as discussed below) in the privacy of one's own home.[17] There is, however, no corollary privacy right that accompanies a person into public places, including while using an interactive computer, to acquire obscene material.[18] Neither is there a defense for displaying or distributing obscenity to consenting adults.[19]

The Legal Test

The three-prong test for determining obscenity is a composite of the Supreme Court's decisions in *Miller, Smith v. United States*,[20] and *Pope v. Illinois*:[21]

1. Whether the average person, applying contemporary adult community standards, would find that the work, taken as a whole, appeals to the prurient interest (i.e., an erotic, lascivious, abnormal, unhealthy, degrading, shameful, or morbid interest in nudity, sex, or excretion); **and**

2. Whether the average person, applying contemporary adult community standards, would find that the work depicts or describes, in a patently offensive way, sexual conduct (i.e., ultimate sexual acts, normal or perverted, actual or simulated; masturbation; excretory functions; lewd exhibition of the genitals; or sadomasochistic sexual abuse); **and**

3. Whether a reasonable person would find that the work, taken as a whole, lacks serious literary, artistic, political, or scientific value.

In *Miller*, the Supreme Court stated that any material that depicts or describes "hard-core sexual conduct" can be found obscene. The Court's examples of such conduct were set out in *Miller* as "ultimate sexual acts, normal or perverted, actual or simulated," and "masturbation, excretory functions, and lewd exhibitions of the genitals."[22]

The term *hard-core pornography* is commonly used to refer to material that shows penetration clearly visible. This explicit type of pornography has been widely held by courts as material that clearly fits within the definition of obscenity and lacks First Amendment protection.

To convict someone of trafficking in obscenity, the

law does not require proof that the person accused made a legal determination that the material is obscene. All that's required is proof that the person knew the general nature or character of the material[23]—that it is sexually explicit.

Because of the way in which hard-core porn is described in advertising, it's easy to understand why proving the accused's knowledge of the material is not difficult. Phrases like "XXX hard-core," "girls who take it in the a**," "f***-fest," "1001 cum shots," and others so vulgar and graphic we won't include them here, are used to describe and promote hard-core porn. The porn industry is guilty of many wrongs, but not of false advertising and product puffing. Generally, what pornographers advertise is what they provide.

If you see or receive unsolicited material that meets the definition of obscenity, do not store it on a computer or computer disk. It should be reported immediately to local law enforcement and the FBI. If it was sent through the mail, it should be taken to a U.S. postal inspector.

Child Pornography

Child porn is the most deplorable form of pornography because it involves the rape, sodomy, or other sexual abuse of a child. It is a crime-scene photograph and nothing less. It's illegal under federal and most state laws to possess, acquire, produce, distribute, copy, or display.[24] Under federal law, there is no requirement that child porn must be obscene under the *Miller* test.[25]

Again under federal law, child pornography is

defined as a visual depiction of a minor child engaged in actual or simulated sexual conduct, including a lascivious exhibition of the genitals or pubic area.[26] Federal law defines a minor as a person under the age of 18 years.[27] If a photograph depicts someone who is obviously a minor engaged in a sex act or a lascivious exhibition of the genitals, it is contraband that may be seized on sight by law enforcement.

Photos that depict mere nudity,[28] such as innocent photos generally taken by parents or grandparents of a baby lying on a rug with his or her bare bottom in view, do not constitute child pornography. On the other hand, nudity is not required in order to violate child pornography laws.[29] The determining factors are:

1. whether the focal point of the visual depiction is the child's genitalia or pubic area;

2. whether the setting of the visual depiction is sexually suggestive, that is, in a place or pose generally associated with sexual activity;

3. whether the child is depicted in an unnatural pose, or in inappropriate attire, considering the age of the child;

4. whether the child is fully or partially clothed, or nude;

5. whether the visual depiction suggests sexual coyness or a willingness to engage in sexual activity;

6. whether the visual depiction is intended or designed to elicit a sexual response in the viewer.

Of course, a visual depiction need not involve all these factors to be a lascivious exhibition of the genitals or pubic area. The determination will have to be made based on the overall content of the visual depiction, taking into account the age of the minor.[30]

If you see or receive unsolicited child pornography via the Internet or through E-mail, don't store the material on a computer hard drive or disk. It should be reported immediately to local law enforcement and the FBI, along with any information regarding the source of the material. Individuals who have been found with child porn stored on their computer or computer disks, who claimed to be doing research for writing an article or for assisting law enforcement, have been convicted of violating federal law, and the convictions have been upheld.

The American Civil Liberties Union (ACLU) takes the position that once child pornography photos are made, they constitute "speech" or "expressive conduct" that should be protected by the First Amendment.

Even if we assume for the sake of argument, however, that child porn photos are "speech," it is compelled "speech" that violates the exploited child's First Amendment rights. Children are forced or coerced into sexual conduct by adults who provide them with gifts, money, or attention. Even when a child allegedly "consents," the law does not recognize it because children are mentally and psychologically incapable of making a knowing, intelligent, and voluntary consent.

The ACLU also argues that because it isn't illegal to possess or distribute the photographs of a murder, it shouldn't be illegal to possess or distribute child pornography. That's a flawed argument for several reasons.

First, the First Amendment does not provide a defense to an otherwise criminal act.[31] It's a crime to murder or have someone murdered for the purpose of producing or possessing photos of the murder; the photos would be evidence of the crime.

Second, even if a person who possessed photos of a murder had nothing to do with the murder itself, possession of the photos would not cause the murder victim to suffer any further injury. The same is not true of a sexually abused and photographed child who continues to suffer psychological harm from knowing that the photos exist and someone may see them. The Supreme Court recognized this in *Ferber*.[32] Furthermore, molesters often use the photos to blackmail the child into silence. The child also suffers an atrocious invasion of privacy every time someone looks at the photos. No one has a First Amendment right to violate a child's right to privacy.

Third, mere possession of photos of a murder is highly unlikely to arouse a murderous instinct in the one who possesses them that would result in the commission of other murders for the purpose of photographing them. That is not true of pedophiles, whose insatiable desire for sex with children is fueled by viewing child pornography that, in turn, fuels the desire for more sex with additional children and a desire for more child porn. In *Osborne v. Ohio*,[33] the Supreme Court upheld a state law that criminalized the mere possession of child pornography because the Court recognized that the production of the material is driven by the market for it.

Material Harmful to Minors

Material harmful to minors is also known as "variable obscenity" and is defined by the "*Millerized Ginsberg* Test."[34] In *Ginsberg v. New York*,[35] the Supreme Court said, "Because of the State's exigent interest in preventing distribution to children of objectionable material, it can exercise its power to protect the health, safety, welfare and morals of its community by barring the distribution to children of books recognized to be suitable for adults."

It is illegal under most state laws to sell, exhibit, or display "harmful" (soft-core) pornography to minor children, even if the material is not obscene or illegal for adults.[36] Some state harmful to minors laws apply only to commercial display or distribution. Some laws exempt public libraries and legitimate scientific, educational, or law enforcement purposes, as well as the parent or guardian of a minor child who displays it to his or her child.

A federal harmful to minors law, the Child Online Protection Act (COPA), was enacted October 21, 1998. COPA prohibits "an individual or entity from: knowingly and with knowledge of the character of the material, in interstate or foreign commerce by means of the World Wide Web, making any communication for commercial purposes that is available to any minor and that includes any material that is harmful to minors." A federal district court granted the ACLU a preliminary injunction preventing enforcement of COPA,[37] which was upheld by the Court of Appeals for the Third Circuit.[38] The Supreme Court is reviewing the Third

Circuit's ruling. A trial on the merits of the case is pending the Court's decision. In the meantime, children who have access to the Internet are a few mouse clicks away from full color images of all types of pornography.

"Harmful to minors" means any written, visual, or audio matter of any kind that:

(1) the average person, applying contemporary community standards, would find, taken as a whole and with respect to minors, appeals to a prurient interest in nudity, sex, or excretion; **and**

(2) the average person, applying contemporary community standards, would find depicts, describes, or represents, in a patently offensive way with respect to what is suitable for minors, ultimate sexual acts, normal or perverted, actual or simulated, sado-masochistic sexual acts or abuse, or lewd exhibitions of the genitals, pubic area, buttocks, or post-pubertal female breast; **and**

(3) a reasonable man would find, taken as a whole, lacks serious literary, artistic, political, or scientific value for minors.[39]

Most states have laws that require "blinder racks" for the display of material harmful to minors in public places to which minors have access, so that the lower two-thirds of the cover is not visible. Some state laws do not require "blinder racks" but permit cities and counties to enact ordinances that require them. Some states require that in order to protect minors, the material must be sealed in cellophane or kept in an area for "adults only."

Broadcast Indecency

Broadcast indecency is defined by the Federal Communications Commission (FCC) as "language or material that, in context, depicts or describes in terms patently offensive as measured by contemporary community standards for the broadcast medium, sexual or excretory activities or organs." George Carlin's infamous "Seven Dirty Words" were the subject of the U.S. Supreme Court case *FCC v. Pacifica Foundation*.[40]

Broadcast indecency regulations are enforced by the FCC from 6 A.M. to 10 P.M. A complaint alleging a broadcast of indecency during the prohibited time period should be filed with the FCC. The complaint must contain the name of the program, the date and time of the broadcast, and a tape recording of the program. Recently, however, the FCC accepted a complaint without requiring a recording of the program.

Dial-a-Porn

Dial-a-porn is "the description or depiction of sexual or excretory activities or organs in a patently offensive manner as measured by contemporary community standards for the telephone medium." To receive it, the law requires a written request from an adult, a credit card number, or an adult identification PIN code before transmission.[41] Obscene dial-a-porn is illegal to transmit to anyone, however, regardless of consent.

A phone subscriber who has not placed a written request for dial-a-porn services and is confident that no one else in the household has done so, but who finds a charge for such service on his telephone bill, should dispute payment and report the dial-a-porn provider to the FCC and the U.S. Department of Justice.

Cable Indecency

Cable indecency "describes or depicts sexual or excretory activities or organs in a patently offensive manner as measured by contemporary community standards for the cable medium." Cable operators may refuse to carry indecent leased-access programming that the operator reasonably believes meets that definition. Cable operators who choose to carry indecent programming on leased-access channels are *not* required to place such programs on a separate channel and block the channel until the subscriber, in writing, requests unblocking.

Cable operators may not prohibit the use of PEG-access channels (Public-Education-Government) for "any programming which contains obscene material, sexually explicit conduct, or material soliciting or promoting unlawful conduct."[42] That does not, however, shield the programmer from being prosecuted for disseminating obscenity.

In *U.S. v. Playboy Entertainment Group, Inc.,*[43] the Supreme Court upheld 47 U.S.C. § 560. This federal statute requires cable television operators who provide channels primarily dedicated to sexually oriented programming to fully scramble or otherwise fully block both the audio and video signals of those channels from the homes of cable subscribers who do not subscribe to the programming and who request total blocking. This must done by the cable company at no cost to the subscriber.

Sexually Oriented Advertising

Sexually oriented mail ads may be blocked from your residence if you file forms available at the post office with the local postmaster. The applicable law is 39 USCS § 3010 (2000):

Mailing of sexually oriented advertisements

(a) Any person who mails or causes to be mailed any sexually oriented advertisement shall place on the envelope or cover thereof his name and address as the sender thereof and such mark or notice as the Postal Service may prescribe.

(b) Any person, on his own behalf or on the behalf of any of his children who has not attained the age of 19 years and who resides with him or is under his care, custody, or supervision, may file with the Postal Service a statement, in such form and manner as the Postal Service may prescribe, that he desires to receive no sexually oriented advertisements through the mails. The Postal Service shall maintain and keep current, insofar as practicable, a list of the names and addresses of such persons and shall make the list (including portions thereof or changes therein) available to any person, upon such reasonable terms and conditions as it may prescribe, including the payment of such service charge as it determines to be necessary to defray the cost of compiling and maintaining the list and making it available as provided in this sentence. No person shall mail

264 • *Protecting Your Child in an X-Rated World*

or cause to be mailed any sexually oriented advertisement to any individual whose name and address has been on the list for more than 30 days.

(c) No person shall sell, lease, lend, exchange, or license the use of, or, except for the purpose expressly authorized by this section, use any mailing list compiled in whole or in part from the list maintained by the Postal Service pursuant to this section.

(d) "Sexually oriented advertisement" means any advertisement that depicts, in actual or simulated form, or explicitly describes, in a predominantly sexual context, human genitalia, any act of natural or unnatural sexual intercourse, any act of sadism or masochism, or any other erotic subject directly related to the foregoing. Material otherwise within the definition of this subsection shall be deemed not to constitute a sexually oriented advertisement if it constitutes only a small and insignificant part of the whole of a single catalog, book, periodical, or other work the remainder of which is not primarily devoted to sexual matters.

Sexually Oriented Businesses

Sexually oriented businesses may be regulated by content-neutral time, place, and manner licensing and zoning laws in order to protect children, residential areas, schools, libraries, youth clubs, religious institutions, and other sensitive uses from the adverse secondary effects of such businesses.[44] Land use studies from more than 30 cities across the country have documented the harmful secondary effects caused by sexually oriented businesses. Those effects include increased crime; decreased property values and tax revenue; spread of sexually transmitted diseases; sexual harassment; urban blight; littering of pornographic materials, used hypodermic needles, and used condoms; and increased traffic, noise, and cruising.

Coercion and Enticement of a Minor for Prostitution

Coercing or enticing a minor by using the mail or interstate or foreign commerce for the purpose of engaging in sexual conduct is punishable under federal law:

18 U.S.C. § 2422:

(a) Whoever knowingly persuades, induces, entices, or coerces any individual to travel in interstate or foreign commerce, or in any Territory or Possession of the United States, to engage in prostitution, or in any sexual activity for which any person can be charged with a criminal offense, or attempts to do so, shall be fined under this title or imprisoned not more than 10 years, or both.

(b) Whoever, using the mail or any facility or means of interstate or foreign commerce, or within the special maritime and territorial jurisdiction of the United States knowingly persuades, induces, entices, or coerces any individual who has not attained the age of 18 years, to engage in prostitution or any sexual activity for which any person can be charged with a criminal offense, or attempts to do so, shall be fined under this title, imprisoned not more than 15 years, or both.

If you or your child receives a message as defined in

subsections (a) or (b) through the mail, via electronic mail, or while participating in an Internet chat room, you should report it to local law enforcement, the U.S. Postal Service (for regular mail), and the FBI.

Transportation of Minors for Prostitution or Sexual Activity

Transporting minors for prostitution or other sexual activity is also prohibited under federal law:

18 U.S.C. § 2423:

(a) Transportation with intent to engage in criminal sexual activity. A person who knowingly transports an individual who has not attained the age of 18 years in interstate or foreign commerce, or in any commonwealth, territory or possession of the United States, with intent that the individual engage in prostitution, or in any sexual activity for which any person can be charged with a criminal offense, or attempts to do so, shall be fined under this title, imprisoned not more than 15 years, or both.

(b) Travel with intent to engage in sexual act with a juvenile. A person who travels in interstate commerce, or conspires to do so, or a United States citizen or an alien admitted for permanent residence in the United States who travels in foreign commerce, or conspires to do so, for the purpose of engaging in any sexual act (as defined in section 2246) with a person under 18 years of age that would be in violation of chapter 109A [18 USCS §§ 2241 et seq.] if the sexual act occurred in the special maritime and territorial jurisdiction of the

United States shall be fined under this title, imprisoned not more than 15 years, or both.

Pedophiles have traveled cross-country and into the U.S. from other countries in order to have sex with minor children they have encountered on the Internet. In addition, minor children have unwittingly traveled across the country to meet a new "friend" (pedophile) who has provided a plane or bus ticket. Children should be warned that they should never give out personal information on the Internet and should never arrange to meet someone without parental knowledge and consent. If a minor child receives a request to meet with someone unknown to the parents, who knows or should know that the child is a minor, the incident should be reported to local law enforcement and the FBI.

Finally, any questions regarding a particular state's pornography laws should be directed to the local prosecuting attorney's office, as laws vary from state to state.

APPENDIX B

Resources

⋖⁘⋗

One of the best ways you can protect your child in an X-rated world is to be informed about the issue of pornography and *stay* informed. Rapid change is the norm on the Internet, and local, federal, and state laws also change frequently. We understand the burden this places on you, but what's the alternative?

In this age of cyberporn, the gay rights movement, and Planned Parenthood/SIECUS-based sex education, parenting has never been more difficult or challenging. Your child today faces dangers that no one saw back in the 1950s, when the Baby Boom generation was growing up. In those calmer, more sane times, premarital sex was universally condemned. A girl who became pregnant either married or put her child up for adoption. Today, premarital sex can result not only in a baby, an abortion, or STDs, but also in AIDS infection and death

269

of one or both participants. Yet despite the risk of catching an incurable disease that can kill a sex-charged teen, groups like Planned Parenthood actively *promote* physical intimacy before marriage.

Something is wrong with this picture. It all goes back to the philosophy of pornography that we discussed earlier. We're not simply debating with people who are misinformed and naive about the consequences of children being sexualized and addicted to porn at an early age. The porn pushers *want* your child to become hooked because many kids become lifelong buyers of pornography. Many pro-abortion groups *want* abortions because that's how they make their money. In a perverse way, many gay activists exploit AIDS because the more AIDS sufferers there are, the more money they can get from the federal government to fund "AIDS education" programs in the public schools. Regrettably, most of these programs are just thinly disguised recruitment programs that may lead sexually confused children into a sex addiction and AIDS infection.

These are just a few of the reasons why you are wise to guard your child and home from the infection of the pornography virus. And they are also why you need to keep up to date on the latest mutations of this virus and how it may find other ways to invade your home. The list of resources below isn't exhaustive, but it will give you a good start as you continue to work at understanding the dangers of pornography as it increasingly permeates our society. *Inclusion on this list does not necessarily constitute endorsement of material, content, or organizational viewpoint by the publisher or authors of this book.*

FAMILY-FRIENDLY INTERNET SERVICE/FILTERING PROVIDERS

New companies providing Internet service are started every day, it seems, while others that have been available go out of business. Likewise, new filtering programs regularly come on the market, while others are withdrawn. Any list of such companies and products that we might provide here would be outdated before the book came off the press. To get up-to-date information on family-friendly Internet service providers and filtering programs, Focus on the Family recommends that you access www.filterreview.com, a resource operated by the National Coalition for the Protection of Children and Families. You may also want to visit the tools section of the Web site www.GetNetWise.org, a service of the Internet Education Foundation.

ANTI-PORNOGRAPHY/ANTI-GAY ACTIVIST GROUPS

Many of these groups deal with pornography exclusively, while others confront this issue as well as many other anti-child, anti-family social forces in our society. As you access their Web sites, you'll see the issues they confront.

American Decency Association (ADA)
ADA is a Christian group dedicated to fighting pornography through education and boycotts. ADA has targeted the advertisers of Howard Stern's radio and TV programs,

among others. It has convinced hundreds of sponsors to drop their advertising support of Stern's indecent programming. For more information, go to www.american-decency.org. Write or call: ADA, P.O. Box 202, Fremont, MI 49412-0202; 231/924-4050; E-mail: info@american-decency.org.

American Family Association (AFA)

AFA is one of the most aggressive and effective activist organizations in the country. Under the leadership of the Rev. Donald Wildmon, AFA has confronted the pornography industry, the gay rights movement, sexually explicit television programming, and more. AFA has a radio network, daily news service, monthly magazine, and E-mail alerts. It also offers a filtered Internet service called American Family Online. For more information, access www.afa.net or write AFA, P.O. Drawer 2440, Tupelo, MS 38803.

Amy's Friends

Amy Dupree, a former stripper, founded this ministry to help free girls from the bondage of the sex club business. Amy's Friends provides spiritual and physical care for women who seek to leave the strip club scene and live productive, God-honoring lives. The group has a mentoring program and shows concerned citizens how they can set up Amy's Friends chapters in their own communities. For more details on this important outreach, access www.amysfriends.org, or write or call or E-mail: 214/965-9666; cpool@amysfriends.org.

Citizens for Community Values (CCV)

This group is a major player in the battle against pornography and the normalization of homosexuality in our culture. CCV's stated mission is to "promote Judeo-Christian moral values and to reduce destructive behaviors contrary to those values" through education, activism, and the empowerment of individuals at the local and national level. CCV conducts seminars on pornography, homosexuality, obscenity law enforcement, and more. To learn about CCV's work, access: www.ccv.org, or write or call: Citizens for Community Values, 11175 Reading Road, Suite 103, Cincinnati, OH 45241-1997; 513/733-5775; E-mail: info@ccv.org.

Concerned Women for America (CWA)

CWA is the largest women's group in the United States. Founded by Beverly LaHaye, CWA boasts a membership of more than 600,000. It publishes a monthly newsletter and special reports, issues action alerts, and maintains a searchable Web site. CWA's primary concerns are: homosexuality, abortion, feminism, children, and parenting. For more details, access www.cwfa.org. Write or call: CWA, 1015 Fifteenth Street, NW, Suite 1100, Washington, D.C. 20005; 202/488-7000.

Enough Is Enough! (EIE)

The mission of this group is to "greatly reduce sexual violence and to prevent children, women, men and families from becoming victims by eliminating child pornography and removing hard-core and illegal pornography from the marketplace." EIE has a Web site, publishes a newsletter, and offers an action manual for cleaning up communities. For more information, write or call Enough Is Enough!, P.O. Box 26228, Santa Ana, CA 92799-6228; 888/2ENOUGH; or access their Web site: www.enough.org.

Family Friendly Libraries (FFL)
In 2000, FFL became a division of Citizens for Community Values. FFL's goal is to promote a safe environment for children and adults in public and school libraries. FFL believes library computers should have filters on them to protect children from exposure to sexual images. FFL also believes the library should be a safe haven from child molesters and potential rapists who are increasingly taking control of library computers to view pornographic materials. FFL has an excellent Web site that gives concerned parent activists strategies for approaching their local librarians about Internet porn and other sexually explicit materials in our nation's libraries. Access www.fflibraries.org, and write or call Family Friendly Libraries, 11175 Reading Road, Suite 103, Cincinnati, OH 45141; 513/733-8908.

Family Research Council (FRC)
This Washington, D.C.-based group plays a leading role in fighting pornography, the gay rights movement, abortion, the feminization of the military, the destruc-

tion of the family, and so on. FRC maintains a searchable database on its Web site, publishes excellent research papers on porn and a variety of other social issues, and encourages citizen activism. For more information, write or call: FRC, 801 G Street, NW, Washington, DC 20001; 202/393-2100; Web site: www.frc.org.

Focus on the Family (FOF)

FOF is a well-known leader in the pro-family movement. Founder Dr. James Dobson was on the Attorney General's Commission on Pornography in 1985-86 and helped craft the *Final Report of the Attorney General's Commission on Pornography* for President Reagan's attorney general, Edwin Meese. FOF's public policy department produces *Citizen* magazine, a weekly E-mail update called *Citizen Issues Alert,* "Family News in Focus" (a daily radio program), and research papers dealing with pornography, gambling, homosexuality, and more. FOF also maintains a Web site featuring CitizenLink and PureIntimacy.com, a site providing help for pornography addicts. Access the Focus Web site at www.fotf.org, or write or call FOF at Focus on the Family, Colorado Springs, CO 80995; 719/531-3400.

Morality in Media (MIM)

One of the oldest antipornography groups in the nation, MIM is an interfaith group committed to public education and legal assistance in fighting pornography. It is also involved in efforts to fight the erosion of decency

standards in our culture. MIM sponsors the White
Ribbon Campaign Against Pornography and the
National Turn Off TV Day each year. Its National
Obscenity Law Center (NOLC) is a clearinghouse of
information on obscenity law and provides legal counsel to groups fighting pornography in their communities. For more information on MIM, access their Web
site: www.moralityinmedia.org. Write or call: Morality
in Media, 475 Riverside Drive, New York, NY 10115;
212/870-3222.

National Coalition for the Protection of Children & Families (NCPCF)

NCPCF's stated goal is to "empower concerned citizens
and community leaders to significantly reduce sexual
exploitation and violence in America by: Increasing
public awareness of the availability and harm of
exploitative and abusive pornography, particularly in
the lives of children; Supporting the enactment and
enforcement, within the Constitution, of limitations on
pornography; Offering assistance to people harmed by
pornography." For more details on their work, access
their Web site, www.nationalcoalition.org, or write or
call: NCPCF, 800 Compton Road, Suite 9224, Cincinnati, OH 45231; 513/521-6227.

National Law Center for Children and Families (NLC)

This group provides legal advice and training for law
enforcement officers and citizen activists in dealing
with the pornography plague in their communities.

Bruce A. Taylor, the president and chief counsel at the time of this writing, has been fighting porn for more than two decades and worked in the Reagan Justice Department, fighting obscenity. The NLC has published proposed guidelines for libraries to use in keeping pornography off library computers, plus materials on regulating sexually oriented businesses. To contact the NLC, access: www.NationalLawCenter.org, or write or call: National Law Center for Children and Families, 3919 Plaza Drive, Fairfax, VA 22030-2512; 703/691-4626.

Traditional Values Coalition (TVC)

This Washington, D.C.-based organization represents the interests of 43,000 churches. Founded by the Rev. Louis P. Sheldon, TVC's primary concerns are: religious freedom, the gay rights movement, abortion (including partial-birth abortion), and pornography. The group directly lobbies members of Congress; publishes a monthly newsletter, special reports, and E-mail alerts; and maintains a Web site with a searchable database. For more information, access www.traditionalvalues.org. Write or call: TVC, 139 C Street, SE, Washington, DC 20003; 202/547-8570; E-mail: tvcwashdc@traditionalvalues.org.

Victims of Pornography

This is a campaign, not an organization. Its Web site will provide you with statistics, testimonies, and strategies for fighting pornography in your community. Access www.victimsofpornography.org.

PARENT'S RIGHTS GROUPS/LEGAL DEFENSE

Alliance Defense Fund (ADF)
Currently headed by constitutional attorney Alan Sears, ADF is a Christian legal group dedicated to the court room defense of religious freedom, family values, and the sanctity of human life. Contact them at: www.alliancedefensefund.org; 8960 Raintree Dr., Suite 300, Scottsdale, AZ 85260; 800/TELL-ADF.

American Center for Law and Justice (ACLJ)
The ACLJ is a not-for-profit public-interest law firm and educational organization dedicated to the promotion of pro-liberty, pro-life, and pro-family causes. It is also developing a national network of attorneys committed to the defense of religious and civil liberties. Web site: www.aclj.org. Write or call: P.O. Box 64429, Virginia Beach, VA 23467; 757/226-2489.

Becket Fund for Religious Liberty
The Becket Fund is a nonpartisan, ecumenical, public-interest law firm that defends the civil rights of people from all religious traditions. Web site: www.becket-fund.org. Write or call: 1350 Connecticut Ave., Suite 605, Washington, DC 20036; 800/BECKET-5.

Catholic League for Religious and Civil Rights
This largest Catholic civil-rights organization in the U.S. works to safeguard the religious freedom and free-

speech rights of Catholics wherever they're threatened. The League is a lay organization, not an official arm of the Catholic church. Web site: www.catholicleague.org. Write or call: 450 Seventh Ave., New York, NY 10023; 212/371-3191.

Gateways to Better Education

This national nonprofit Christian ministry is dedicated to giving parents the tools and techniques to get the best education they can from public schools and assure that their children grow spiritually strong, morally sound, and academically accomplished. They offer telephone counseling, a parent network, a newsletter, and other unique resources. Web site: www.gtbe.org. Write or call: P.O. Box 514, Lake Forest, CA 92609; 949/586-5437.

Home School Legal Defense Association (HSLDA)

HSLDA provides low-cost legal advice for families that home-school. Parents pay $100 per year for membership and are defended free of charge should the necessity arise. Web site: www.hslda.org. Write or call: P.O. Box 3000, Purcelleville, VA 20134-9000; 540/338-5600.

Legal Facts

This is not an organization but a weekly publication produced by co-author Jan LaRue for the Family Research Council. *Legal Facts* is an excellent resource to keep you up to date on the latest legal challenges facing parents, children, and Christians. This activist-oriented newsletter is available by E-mail, or it can be down-loaded free from FRC's Web site. To see *Legal Facts* online, access www.frc.org and search on "legal facts."

Liberty Counsel

Liberty Counsel is a nonprofit religious civil-liberties and legal-defense organization. Web site: www.liberty-counsel.org. Write or call: P.O. Box 540774, Orlando, FL 32854; 407/875-2100.

Pacific Justice Institute (PJI)

This organization offers free legal assistance to parents who find their parental and religious freedom rights being violated. PJI has defended several cases in California involving explicit sex education and the gay rights movement's efforts to recruit children in the public schools. Web site: www.pacificjustice.org. Write or call: 6060 Sunrise Vista Dr., Citrus Heights, CA 95611; 916/857-6900.

The Pro-Family Law Center

This law firm focuses its efforts exclusively on protecting parents and children from homosexual recruitment efforts. It offers a Web site, a newsletter, and special reports. One of its first publications is *Why and How to Defeat the "Gay" Movement.* Web site: www.abidingtruth.com. Write or call: Abiding Truth Ministries, 6060 Sunrise Vista Dr., Suite 3050, Citrus Heights, CA 95610; 916/676-1057.

PRO-FAMILY SEX EDUCATION GROUPS

A number of organizations are working to equip adolescents with effective tools for abstaining from sexual activity.

Abstinence the Better Choice
2222 Issaquah Street
Cuyahoga Falls, OH 44221-3704
Phone: 330/940-4240

Abstinence the Better Choice directs its efforts toward two age groups. The two-week elementary curriculum centers on character development/education and resistance skills in saying no to drugs, alcohol, and sexual involvement. The middle school curriculum focuses primarily on abstinence and provides peer group meetings.

Best Friends
4455 Connecticut Ave., NW, Suite 310
Washington, D.C. 20008
Phone: 202/237-8156
Fax: 202/822-9276
www.bestfriendsfoundation.org

Best Friends is a mentoring program targeted specifically for girls in middle school through high school. The program's success depends on the commitment level of the school guidance counselors or the mentors themselves. It focuses on abstinence and other issues that high school girls face, such as self-esteem, relationships, career goals, and peer pressure.

Choices
Priscilla Hurley
2545 Chapman Ave., suite 220
Fullerton, CA 92831
Phone: 714/523-5997
Fax: 714-525-5753

Targeted at junior and senior high school students, this program focuses on teen sexuality/abstinence. It also provides parents with information on sexual awareness. Presented in a classroom setting for five days, seminars are held in Orange, Los Angeles, and Riverside counties in Southern California.

Focus on the Family
Educational Resources
P.O. Box 15379
Colorado Springs, CO 80935-3579
Phone: 800/932-9123

Focus on the Family distributes *No Apologies: the truth about life, love & sex,* and *Sex, Lies & ... the Truth,* 30-minute videos for junior and senior high school students. The curriculum is available in both public school and Christian versions and may be accompanied by a study guide for classroom or group instruction.

Friends First
Lisa Rue and Joneen Krauth
P.O. Box 356

Longmont, CO 80502
Phone: 303/776-0715
Fax: 303/776-0705
www.friendsfirst.org

Friends First provides a number of services to schools, parents, and the community including "WAIT Training," an in-class abstinence instruction course. Friends First clubs provide peer mentoring and a network of speakers and resources.

Love and Life at the Movies
Onalee McGraw, Ph.D.
188 Berbuse Lane
Front Royal, VA 22630
Phone: 540/635-4420

This institute provides resources and information on healthy sexuality education to parents and schools. It also provides the manual "Foundations for Family Life Education," which gives clear guidelines for family-centered sexuality education. Dr. McGraw recently finished the program "Love and Marriage at the Movies: Educating for Character Through the Film Classics."

Project Reality
Kathleen Sullivan
P.O. Box 97
Golf, IL 60029-0097

284 · *Protecting Your Child in an X-Rated World*

Phone: 847/729-3298

www.projectreality.org

"Choosing the Best," a curriculum for junior and senior high school students, is being piloted by Project Reality in 50 Illinois schools at the time of this writing. The program combines components of *Sex, Lies & ... the Truth,* 17 slides on STDs from the Medical Institute for Sexual Health, and parts of the "No Second Chance" video with Kathy Kay.

Sex, Love and Choices

Sheri Smith, RN

Right to Life League of Southern California

1028 N. Lake Avenue, Suite 104

Pasadena, CA 91104

Phone: 626/398-6100

www.rtllsc.org

Sex, Love and Choices speaks both to junior and senior high school students on public and private campuses with the abstinence message. The presentations consist of a panel of speakers describing personal experiences and the importance of abstinence until marriage as a healthy, livable choice.

Teen Aid

723 E. Jackson

Spokane, WA 99207

Phone: 509/482-2868

www.teen-aid.org

Targeted at junior and senior high school students,

Teen Aid offers an informative course on HIV, as well as a character-based sex education program.

True Love Waits
Southern Baptist Sunday School Board
127 Ninth Avenue N
Nashville, TN 37234
Information: 800/LUV-WAIT
www.lifeway.com

True Love Waits created a national stir when thousands of teens pledged sexual abstinence until marriage. True Love Waits has gone international with its message and continues to provide materials for interested churches and youth groups.

Youth Solutions
Northwest Family Services
4805 NE Glisan Street
Portland, OR 97213
Phone: 503/215-6377

FACTS is an abstinence program for junior and senior high school students with a strong component for parental involvement. It can be used in both public and private schools, and in the community as well.

Speakers

Jeffrey Dean
Wait on Love
225 Cumberland Circle

Nashville, TN 37214
Phone: 615/884-8333
www.jeffreydean.org

Wait on Love offers a message of hope for today's youth. Its goal is to promote and reclaim in youth a positive self-image by encouraging responsible and self-disciplined decisions that overcome negative peer pressure. This program restores a sense of renewed opportunity in youth who have previously made unwise choices. Jeffery Dean uses contemporary/alternative music to relate to teens.

Laurie Stewart
L. A. Stewart Presentations
P.O. Box 50869
Kalamazoo, MI 49005-0869
Phone: 616/372-3200

Laurie Stewart speaks to middle school and high school students across the U.S. and Canada on the issues of abstinence and self-esteem. Presentations include "Back Seat or Honeymoon Suite: You Choose" and "Attitude Check: Being Real, Being Respectful, Being You."

Pat Socia
Freedom Road
P.O. Box 105
Frankston, TX 75763

Phone: 903/586-6236

Pat Socia is a national abstinence speaker who speaks in public junior and senior high school assemblies and at conferences and youth gatherings.

PROFESSIONAL COUNSELING/SEXUAL ADDICTION GROUPS

Bethesda Workshops

These intensive workshops are exclusively for women with sex addictions. A workshop is usually held in a retreat setting from Wednesday through Sunday and consists of lectures, writing assignments, group processing, and worship. The workshops are hosted by Marnie C. Ferree, a licensed marriage and family therapist. As a recovering addict who has been sober for many years, Ferree understands this problem from a personal as well as a professional perspective. Write or call Woodmont Hills Counseling Center, 3710 Franklin Rd., Nashville, TN 37204; 615/269-6220. E-Mail: mferree@bethesdaworkshops.org.

Christians for Sexual Integrity (CSI)

Dr. Robert Jackson, president of CSI, is a licensed psychologist who has treated hundreds of sex and pornography addicts. Jackson headed up the American Family Association's sexual addiction ministry until it became a separate group called the Christian Alliance for Sexual Recovery; CSI has grown out of that now-defunct group. Jackson's vision is that CSI become an "effective tool for evangelism and discipleship" as individuals find hope in Christ to free themselves from sexual addictions. CSI's primary educational tool is a five-day workshop for adult male sex addicts. CSI seeks to prevent, identify early signs of addiction, and treat those who are addicted or are victims of sexual trauma. To contact CSI, access www.sexualintegrity.org, or write or call 4423 Point Fosdick Dr., Suite 100-7, Gig Harbor, WA 98335; 253/851-7726; E-mail: info@sexualintegrity.org.

Esther Ministries

Esther Ministries provides help for women in relationship with sexually addicted men. It offers intensive counseling workshops that typically run four nights and five days.   Call 877/6-ESTHER (637-8437) or access www.estheronline.org.

Faithful & True Ministries

Dr. Mark R. Laaser is a former co-director with Rob Jackson of the Christian Alliance for Sexual Recovery. Laaser now heads up Mark R. Laaser Consulting, Inc., and helps establish Faithful & True sex addiction support groups in churches. Laaser has written extensively on sexual addiction, with an emphasis on sex addicts within the church and pastorate. He also wrote the book *Talking to Your Kids About Sex: How to Have a Lifetime of Age-Appropriate Conversations with Your Children*. Contact Laaser at: Mark R. Laaser Consulting, Inc., P.O. Box

84, Chanhassen, MN 55317; 952/903-9208; E-mail: mlaaser@aol.com. Faithful & True Ministries Web site: www.faithfulandtrueministries.com.

Focus on the Family

Focus on the Family provides professional counseling and referrals. You can reach Focus by calling 719/531-3400 weekdays, 9:00 A.M. to 4:30 P.M. (MST). You should ask for the counselors' assistant. If a counselor is not immediately available, you can leave your contact information and a counselor will call you back as soon as possible. This one-time counseling service is available at no cost to you.

The Focus staff may also be able to help you find a professional counselor in your region who can provide more in-depth and long-term help. This referral service is also available by calling 719/531-3400 weekdays, 9:00 A.M. to 4:30 P.M. (MST) and asking for the counselors' assistant.

Heart to Heart

This organization features counseling services and resources by Dr. Douglas Weiss, a national lecturer, author, and therapist. Access www.sexaddict.com or call 719/278-3708.

New Life Ministries

This organization offers New Liberty, an intensive, 10-day outpatient program for men with sexual addiction. New Life explains that "as a professional program, it adheres to proven clinical interventions," and "as a Christian program, it remains Christ-centered and biblically uncompromising, with a no-nonsense emphasis on personal responsibility and spiritual growth." Access www.newlife.com or call 800/639-5433.

Dr. Clifford and Joyce Penner

The Penners offer a range of books, tapes, and seminars focused on achieving healthy and fulfilling sexual relationships. They have a useful list of frequently asked questions on their Web site, addressing topics ranging from masturbation to "hum-drum" sex lives. The Penners are the authors of the book *The Gift of Sex*, which is available in the Focus on the Family online resource store. The Penners' Web site: www.passionatecommitment.com.

Stone Gate Ministries

Founded by Dr. Harry W. Schaumburg, author of *False Intimacy: Understanding the Struggle of Sexual Addiction*, Stone Gate features "Brief Intensive Counseling," a unique ministry that has helped more than 900 people in the past six years. Access www.stonegateresources.com, or write or call 11509 Palmer Divide Rd., Larkspur, CO 80118; 303/688-5680.

SUPPORT GROUPS

Support groups often can provide relationships and

resources that are more affordable than intensive counseling. Although confidentiality and the focus on individual needs are less in support groups, participants benefit from knowing they are not alone and from developing accountability relationships.

Women's Groups
COSA (Co-dependents of Sex Addicts)
763/537-6904
www.cosa-recovery.org

S-Anon
615/833-3152

Secular Sex-Addict Support Groups (12-step approach)
Sex Addicts Anonymous
713/869-4902 (M-F, 10 A.M.–6 P.M.)

Sexaholics Anonymous
615/331-6230

Sex and Love Addicts Anonymous
781/255-8825

Christian Hospital Programs
Minirth-Meier New Life
800/NEW-LIFE

Rapha

800/383-HOPE

Books/Booklets/Tapes/Videos on Pornography, Sex Addiction, Gender Identity Disorders, Violence in the Media, Sex Education, Gay Rights Movement, etc.

The Children of Table 34: The True Story Behind Alfred Kinsey's Infamous Sex Research (Washington, D.C.: Family Research Council; video).

Don't Touch That Dial: The Impact of the Media on Children and the Family, by Barbara Hattemer and H. Robert Showers (Lafayette, La.: Huntington House Publishers, 1993; book).

False Intimacy: Understanding the Struggle of Sexual Addiction, by Dr. Harry W. Schaumburg (Colorado Springs, Colo.: NavPress, 1997; book).

Fantasy World: Pure Thinking in a Sea of Unrealistic Images, by Sara June Davis and Lindy Beam, Focus on the Family's Dare 2 Dig Deeper Series, 2000. (booklet)

Final Report of the Attorney General's Commission on Pornography, introduction by Michael J. McManus (Nashville: Rutledge Hill Press, 1986; book).

A Guide to What One Person Can Do About Pornography (Tupelo, Miss.: American Family Association, undated; booklet).

Homosexual Activists Work to Lower the Age of Sexual Consent (Washington, D.C.: Family Research Council, 1999; booklet).

Homosexuality: A Freedom Too Far, by Dr. Charles W. Socarides (Phoenix: Adam Margrave Books, 1995; book).

Homosexuality and the Politics of Truth, by Dr. Jeffrey Satinover (Grand Rapids, Mich.: Baker Book House, 1996; book).

In Your Face ... In Your Mind, by Steve Watters, Focus on the Family's Dare 2 Dig Deeper Series, 2000. (booklet)

Kids Online, by Donna Rice Hughes (Grand Rapids, Mich.: Fleming H. Revell, 1998; book).

Kinsey: Crimes and Consequences, by Judith A. Reisman (Arlington, Va.: The Institute for Media Education, 2000; book).

Kinsey, Sex, and Fraud, by Judith A. Reisman (Lafayette, La.: Huntington House Publishers,1990; book).

The Myths of Sex Education, by Josh McDowell (San Bernardino, Calif.: Here's Life Publishers, 1987; book).

Parents' Guide to the Spiritual Growth of Children, John Trent, Ph.D., Rick Osborne, and Kurt Bruner, general eds. (Wheaton, Ill.: Focus on the Family/Tyndale, 2000; book).

Parents' Guide to the Spiritual Mentoring of Teens, Joe White and Jim Weidmann, general eds. (Wheaton, Ill.: Focus on the Family/Tyndale, 2001; book).

"Porn Nation," by Jan LaRue, in *World and I* magazine, August 2000.

Pornography's Effects on Adults and Children, by Dr. Victor B. Cline (New York: Morality in Media, 1999; booklet).

Pure Desire: How One Man's Triumph Over His Greatest Struggle Can Help Others Break Free, by Ted Roberts (Ventura, Calif.: Gospel Light/Regal Books, 1999; book).

The Rude and the Crude: Profanity in Popular Entertainment (Washington, D.C.: Center for Media and Public Affairs, 1999; booklet).

Send a Message to Mickey, by Dr. Richard Land and Frank York (Nashville: Broadman & Holman Publishers, 1998; book).

Sex, Lies & ... the Truth, by Rolf Zettersten

(Wheaton, Ill.: Living Books, 1994; book).

The Silent War: Ministering to Those Trapped in the Deception of Pornography, by Henry J. Rogers (Green Forest, Ark.: New Leaf Press, 1999; book).

Soul Murder: Are Bad Parenting and the Popular Culture Creating a Generation of Psychopaths?, by Frank York (Washington, D.C.: *Insight*, Family Research Council, 2000; booklet).

Stranger in the House (formerly *TV: The World's Greatest Mind-Bender: A Handbook for a Citizens' Crusade for Decent TV*) (New York: Morality in Media, 1998; booklet).

Talking to Your Kids About Sex, by Dr. Mark Laaser (Colorado Springs, Colo.: WaterBrook Press, 1999; book).

What One Woman Can Do: Take Action Manual (Fairfax, Va.: Enough Is Enough!, 1996; booklet).

When the Wicked Seize a City, by Chuck and Donna McIlhenny, and Frank York (Lincoln, Nebr.: iUniverse.com, 2000; book).

Notes

CHAPTER ONE

1. "The Availability of Obscene Material on the Internet," Hearing of the Telecommunications, Trade and Consumer Protection Subcommittee of the House Commerce Committee, May 23, 2000.
2. "Shocking New Study Calls for Drastic Measures," National Coalition for the Protection of Children and Families," NCPCF Web site: www.national-coalition.org, fall 1999.
3. "Online Victimization: A Report on the Nation's Youth," National Center for Missing and Exploited Children Web site: www.ncmec.org.
4. "Centerfold Syndrome Hurts Relationships," United Press International, August 10, 1996.
5. Kiesa Kay, "Caution! Think Peeks at Porn Can't Hurt? Think Again, One Expert Says," *Chicago Tribune*, May 27, 1997, p. 3.
6. Donna Kato, "Soft Porn: How Men View Real Women After Reading Magazines Found Disturbing," *Calgary Herald*, September 22, 1994, p. B10.

7. "Subtle Dangers of Pornography," Focus on the Family's PureIntimacy.org Web site.

8. Kato, p. B10.

9. Henry J. Rogers, *The Silent War: Ministering to Those Trapped in the Deception of Pornography* (Green Forest, Ark.: New Leaf Press, 2000), p. 17.

10. "Zogby Survey Reveals a Growing Percentage of Those Seeking Sexual Fulfillment on the Internet," Focus on the Family's PureIntimacy.org Web site.

11. "Cybersex Gives Birth to a Psychological Disorder," *The New York Times on the Web*, May 16, 2000.

12. Dr. Victor Cline, *Pornography's Effects on Adults and Children* (New York: Morality in Media, n.d.).

13. *Final Report of the Attorney General's Commission on Pornography* (Nashville: Rutledge Hill Press, 1986), p. xxxi.

14. Dr. Jeffrey Satinover, *Homosexuality and the Politics of Truth* (Grand Rapids, Mich.: Baker Book House, 1996), p. 141.

15. William A. Stanmeyer, *The Seduction of Society: Pornography and Its Impact on American Life* (Ann Arbor, Mich.: Servant Books, 1984), p. 35.

16. "Just Harmless Fun?" Enough Is Enough! Newsletter, Enough.org.

17. Cline, *Pornography's Effects on Adults and Children*, p. 5.

18. Hearing of the Telecommunications, Trade and Consumer Protection Subcommittee of the House Commerce Committee, May 23, 2000.

19. "Ex-Church Worker Admits Molestation," Associated Press, June 22, 2000.

20. "PA Minister Arrested in Net Sex Sting," *The Star-Ledger* (New Jersey), June 29, 2000.

21. "Child Molestation: Danger Lurks Close to Home, *Arizona Republic,* January 26, 2000.

22. "Child Molestation," Enough Is Enough! Web site: www.enough.org/myth.

23. "Rape & Sexual Violence," Enough Is Enough! Web site.

24. "A Guide to What One Person Can Do About Pornography," American Family Association, p. 9.

25. Carroll Lachnitt, "Children Who Molest Children a Growing Trend," *Orange County Register,* October 28, 1991, p. B5.

26. Dianna Marder, "When the Child Molester Is a Child, Too," *Philadelphia Inquirer,* January 17, 1993, p. A1.

27. Kim Hone-McMahan and Ed Meyer, "Children Molesting Children," *Akron Beacon Journal,* January 10, 1999, p. A1.

CHAPTER TWO

1. Dr. Victor Cline, *Pornography's Effects on Adults and Children* (New York: Morality in Media, n.d.), pp. 10-11.

2. David Burt, *Dangerous Access 2000: Uncovering Internet Pornography in America's Libraries,* Family Research Council, Washington, D.C., 2000, p. 1.

3. *TV: The World's Greatest Mind-Bender* (New York: Morality in Media, 1998), p. 3.

CHAPTER THREE

1. "Trampling on Parents' Rights: Everyday Life in Massachusetts," March 9, 2001, www.dadi.org/trample.htm.
2. Donna Rice Hughes, *Kids Online* (Grand Rapids, Mich.: Fleming H. Revell, 1998), pp. 179-80.
3. Accuracy in Academia Web site, www.academia.org, 1999.

CHAPTER FOUR

1. Gregg Lewis, *The Power of a Promise Kept* (Colorado Springs, Colo.: Focus on the Family, 1995), pp. 116-17.
2. Ted Roberts, *Pure Desire* (Ventura, Calif.: Regal Books, 1999), p. 95.
3. Lewis, *The Power of a Promise Kept*, p. 130.
4. Stephen Arterburn, Fred Stoeker, and Mike Yorkey, *Every Man's Battle* (Colorado Springs, Colo.: WaterBrook Press, 2000), p. x.
5. "Statistics on Stepfamilies," Smalley online Web site.
6. Peter Gerlach, "Acknowledge and Guard Against a Weaker Incest Taboo," www.stepfamilyinfo.org Web site.

7. Dr. Archibald Hart, *Helping Children Survive Divorce* (Dallas: Word Publishing, 1996), p. 163.
8. Dr. James Dobson, *Parenting Isn't for Cowards* (Dallas: Word Publishing, 1987), pp. 227-28.

CHAPTER FIVE

1. John Trent, Ph.D., Rick Osborne, and Kurt Bruner, general eds., *Parents' Guide to the Spiritual Growth of Children* (Wheaton, Ill.: Focus on the Family/Tyndale, 2000), p. 27.
2. Dr. Mark Laaser, *Talking to Your Kids about Sex* (Colorado Springs, Colo.: WaterBrook Press, 1999), p. 135.
3. Diane Lore, "Hooked on Cybersex? More and more people are spending hours cruising online sex and chat sites. The public fallout includes the recent porn controversy at the downtown Minneapolis library," *Minneapolis Star Tribune,* May 13, 2000, p. 01E.
4. "Resources for Online Sexual Addiction," February 11, 2000, Focus on the Family, CitizenLink Web site.
5. Sara June Davis and Lindy Beam, *Fantasy World: Pure Thinking in a Sea of Unrealistic Images,* Focus on the Family's Dare 2 Dig Deeper Series, 2000, p. 6.

CHAPTER SIX

1. Tom Minnery, *Pornography: A Human Tragedy* (Wheaton, Ill.: Living Books, Tyndale House Publishers, 1987), pp. 35, 44.
2. "Internet Safety: Building Walls and Building Character," at www.family.org/cforum/feature/a0013496.html.
3. Excerpt found at www.filteringfacts.org.
4. "The Availability of Obscene Material on the Internet," Hearing of the Telecommunications, Trade and Consumer Protection Subcommittee of the House Commerce Committee, May 23, 2000.
5. "Internet Safety: Building Walls and Building Character."
6. "Family-Based Filtered Internet Service Providers," at www.family.org/cforum/research/papersa0002551.html.

CHAPTER SEVEN

1. Steve Gallagher, "Devastated by Internet Porn," from Pure Life Ministries Web site.
2. Dr. Richard Land and Frank York, *Send a Message to Mickey* (Nashville: Broadman & Holman, 1998 pp. 39-44).

CHAPTER EIGHT

1. Joe White and Jim Weidmann, general eds., *Parents' Guide to the Spiritual Mentoring of Teens* (Wheaton, Ill.: Focus on the Family/Tyndale, 2001), p. 296.
2. From a Faithful & True facilitator's manual posted on the Internet at www.helpandhope.org.

APPENDIX A

1. *Miller v. California*, 413 U.S. 15, 18 n. 2 (1973); *Final Report of the Attorney General's Commission on Pornography* (Nashville: Rutledge Hill Press, 1986), chapter 1, "Defining our Central Terms"; *Webster's Dictionary*.
2. *Paris Adult Theatre v. Slaton*, 413 U.S. 49 (1973); *Jenkins v. Georgia*, 418 U.S. 153 (1974); *Erznoznik v. City of Jacksonville*, 422 U.S. 205 (1975).
3. 509 U.S. 544 (1993).
4. *Roth v. United States*, 354 U.S. 476 (1957); *Alberts v. California*, 354 U.S. 476 (1957).
5. *Jacobellis v. Ohio*, 378 U.S. 184, 197 (1964).
6. 383 U.S. 463, 499 (1966).
7. 413 U.S. 15 (1973).
8. 18 U.S.C. §1460.
9. *Id.*, §1461, 1463.
10. *Id.*, §1462.

11. *Id.*, §1464.

12. *Id.*, §1465.

13. *Id.*, §1466.

14. *Id.*, §1468.

15. *Id.*, §1470.

16. *Id.*, §1467.

17. *Stanley v. Georgia*, 394 U.S. 557 (1969).

18. *U.S. v. Thirty-Seven Photographs*, 402 U.S. 363 (1971).

19. *Paris Adult Theatre v. Slaton*, 413 U.S. 49 (1973).

20. 431 U.S. 291, 301-02, 309 (1977).

21. 481 U.S. 497, 500-01 (1987).

22. 413 U.S. at 25 (1973).

23. *Smith v. California*, 361 U.S. 147 (1959).

24. *New York v. Ferber*, 458 U.S. 747 (1982), *Osborne v. Ohio*, 495 U.S. 103 (1990), *U.S. v. X-Citement Video, Inc.*, 513 U.S. 64 (1994). *See also U.S. v. Wiegand*, 812 F.2d 1239 (9th Cir. 1987), *cert. denied*, 484 U.S. 856 (1987); *U.S. v. Knox*, 32 F.3d 733 (3rd Cir. 1994), *cert. denied sub nom Knox v. U.S.*, 513 U.S. 1109 (1995). In 1996, Congress responded to a new threat to children from pedophiles who are using computer technology to produce a new form of child pornography that was not covered under federal law. Congress expanded the definition of child pornography in the Child Pornography Prevention Act of 1996, 18 U.S.C. § 2252A, and § 2256 was amended to include "child pornography" that consists of a visual depiction that "is or appears to be" of an

actual minor engaging in sexually explicit conduct. The Act was upheld in *U.S. v. Mento*, 231
F.3d 912 (4th Cir. 2000); *U.S. v. Acheson*, 195 F.3d
645 (11th Cir. 1999); *U.S. v. Hilton*, 167 F.3d 61,
68-69 (1st Cir. 1999), but struck down *in Free
Speech Coalition v. Reno*, 198 F.3d 1083 (9th Cir.
1999); *cert. granted sub nom Ashcroft v. Free Speech
Coalition*, 121 S. Ct. 876 (2001).

25. *New York v. Ferber*, 458 U.S. 747 (1982).

26. 18 U.S.C. §§2252, 2256.

27. *Id.* §2256.

28. 18 U.S.C. §§ 2252, 2256.

29. *U.S. v. Knox* 32 F.3d 733 (3rd Cir. 1994), *cert.
denied* 115 S. Ct. 897 (1995). (Holding that the
child's genitals need not be visible or even dis-
cernible under clothing for a finding of a lewd or
lascivious exhibition.)

30. *U.S. v. Dost*, 636 F. Supp. 828 (S.D. Cal. 1986),
aff'd U.S. v. Dost, 813 F.2d 1231 (9th Cir. 1987),
See also U.S. v. Wiegand, 812 F.2d 1239 (9th Cir.
1987), *cert. denied*, 484 U.S. 856 (1987).

31. *Massachusetts v. Oakes*, 491 U.S. 576 (1989):
"Soliciting, causing, or encouraging, or permitting
a minor to pose for photographs is no more
speech than is setting a house afire in order to
photograph a burning house." *Id.*, at 610 (Justice
Sandra Day O'Connor).

32. 1) "The states have an interest in 'safeguarding the
physical and psychological well-being of a minor.'"
Ferber, 458 U.S. at 756-757 (1982); 2) "The

depictions are sexually abusive in that they are a permanent record of a child's participation and lead to the creations of networks which foster further exploitation." *Id* at 761; 3) "The advertising and selling of child pornography provides an economic motive for the illegal production of these materials." *Id* at 761; 4) "The value of these depictions is de minimis." *Id* at 762; 5) "Recognition that child pornography is outside the protections of the First Amendment is compatible with decisions making the content of speech sanctionable if the evils of the speech outweigh the expressive interests at stake." *Id* at 763-764.

33. 485 U.S. 203 (1990).
34. *Ginsberg v. New York,* 390 U.S. 629 (1968); and *Miller, Smith, Pope, supra.*
35. 390 U.S. 629 (1968).
36. *Com. of Va. v. Am. Booksellers Ass'n,* 372 S.E.2d 618 (Va. 1988), *followed, American Booksellers Ass'n v. Com. of Va.,* 882 F.2d 125 (4th Cir. 1989), *Crawford v. Lungren,* 96 F.3d 380 (9th Cir. 1996), *cert. denied,* 117 S. Ct. 1249 (1997).
37. *ACLU v. Reno,* 31 F. Supp. 2d 473 (E.D. Pa. 1999).
38. *ACLU v. Reno,* 217 F.3d 162 (3rd Cir. 2000).
39. *Ginsberg v. New York,* 390 U.S. 629 (1968); and *Miller, Smith, Pope, supra.*
40. 438 U.S. 726 (1978). *Action For Children's Television, et al. v. FCC,* 11 F.3d 170, 172 (D.C. Cir. 1993).
41. *Sable Communications of California, Inc. v. FCC,*

492 U.S. 115, 126, 128-30 (1989); *Information Providers' Coalition v. FCC*, 928 F.2d 866, 872 (9th Cir. 1991); *Dial Information Services Corporation of New York v. Thornburgh*, 938 F. 2d 1535 (2nd Cir. 1991), *cert. denied*, 502 U.S. 1072 (1992).

42. *Denver Area Ed. Tel. Consort. v. FCC*, 116 S. Ct. 2374 (1996).

43. _ U.S. _, 120 S. Ct. 1878 (2000).

44. *Young v. American Mini Theatres, Inc.*, 427 U.S. 50, 70, 71 (1976), *Renton v. Playtime Theatres, Inc.*, 475 U.S. 41 (1986).

FOCUS ON THE FAMILY®
Welcome to the Family!

Whether you received this book as a gift, borrowed it from
a friend, or purchased it yourself, we're glad you read it! It's just
one of the many helpful, insightful, and encouraging
resources produced by Focus on the Family.

In fact, that's what Focus on the Family is all about—providing inspiration, information, and biblically based advice to people in all stages of life.

It began in 1977 with the vision of one man, Dr. James Dobson, a licensed
psychologist and author of 16 best-selling books on marriage, parenting,
and family. Alarmed by the societal, political, and economic pressures
that were threatening the existence of the American family, Dr. Dobson
founded Focus on the Family with one employee—an assistant—
and a once-a-week radio broadcast, aired on only 36 stations.

Now an international organization, Focus on the Family is dedicated
to preserving Judeo-Christian values and strengthening the family
through more than 70 different ministries, including eight separate
daily radio broadcasts; television public service announcements;
13 publications; and a steady series of books and award-winning
films and videos for people of all ages and interests.

Recognizing the needs of, as well as the sacrifices and important
contribution made by, such diverse groups as educators, physicians,
attorneys, crisis pregnancy center staff, and single parents,
Focus on the Family offers specific outreaches to uphold and
minister to these individuals, too. And it's all done for one purpose,
and one purpose only: to encourage and strengthen individuals
and families through the life-changing message of Jesus Christ.

• • •

For more information about the ministry, or if we can be of help to your
family, simply write to Focus on the Family, Colorado Springs, CO 80995
or call 1-800-A-FAMILY (1-800-232-6459). Friends in Canada may write
Focus on the Family, P.O. Box 9800, Stn. Terminal, Vancouver, B.C. V6B 4G3
or call 1-800-661-9800. Visit our Web site—www.family.org—
to learn more about Focus on the Family or to find out if
there is an associate office in your country.

We'd love to hear from you!

Creative Correction

Lisa Whelchel, former TV star of "The Facts of Life" and now the mother of three, offers advice for disciplining children in a creative, down-to-earth way. Hardcover.

Parents' Guide to the Spiritual Growth of Children

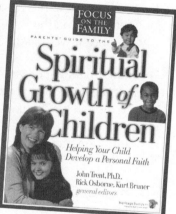

Building a foundation of faith in your children can be easy—and fun!—with help from the *Parents' Guide to the Spiritual Growth of Children.* Through simple and practical advice, this comprehensive guide shows you how to build a spiritual training plan for your family, and it explains what to teach your children at different ages. Hardcover.

• • •

Look for these special books in your Christian bookstore or request a copy by calling 1-800-A-FAMILY (1-800-232-6459). Friends in Canada may write to Focus on the Family, P.O. Box 9800, Stn. Terminal, Vancouver, B.C. V6B 4G3 or call 1-800-661-9800.

Visit our Web site (www.family.org) to learn more about the ministry or to find out if there is a Focus on the Family office in your country.